HEARTFELT
CHANGE

HEARTFELT CHANGE

Turning harmful emotions into positive character

LES CARTER, Ph.D.

MOODY PRESS
CHICAGO

© 1987, 1993 by
LES CARTER

Title of original work:
The Missing Peace: Finding Emotional Balance

All Scripture quotations, unless indicated, are taken from the *New American Standard Bible,* © 1960, 1962, 1963, 1968, 1971, 1972, 1973, 1975, and 1977 by The Lockman Foundation, and are used by permission.

Scripture quotations marked (NIV) are taken from the *Holy Bible: New International Version®.* NIV®. Copyright © 1973, 1978, 1984, International Bible Society. Used by permission of Zondervan Publishing House. All rights reserved.

The use of selected references from various versions of the Bible in this publication does not necessarily imply publisher endorsement of the versions in their entirety.

ISBN: 0-8024-6049-6

1 3 5 7 9 10 8 6 4 2

To my father, Ed Carter.
Thank you for your early support
in my professional growth
and your continued stimulation
of my thinking processes.

CONTENTS

LIST OF ILLUSTRATIONS

My brother, Lee Carter, who practices adolescent psychology in Waco, has been a lifelong supporter and encourager. My father, Ed Carter, has prompted me to think about God's plan for healthy living since I was a boy. Both have played a major role in showing me God's grace.

Finally, thanks go to Trish Turner for her assistance in preparing the manuscript. Her helpful spirit made the project just a little bit easier.

ACKNOWLEDGMENTS

Heartfelt Change is an overview of my concepts of Christian counseling. The ideas expressed are the result of input from many persons much wiser than myself. I am indebted to them for nurturing me in the Lord, pointing me toward a broad understanding of how He works in our emotional and relational lives.

In the fall of 1979, while working at a small clinic in Dallas, I was pleased to meet Frank Minirth to discuss being part of his budding practice. Little did we know how God was going to bless us as the Minirth-Meier Clinic grew to become a nationally known leader in the field of Christian counseling with hundreds of employees. I am grateful to Frank and to Paul Meier for their unwavering commitment to the Word of God as the ultimate resource in the healing of emotional wounds. I am pleased to call them my friends and colleagues.

Other individuals have been influential in stimulating my thinking regarding psychological and spiritual issues. They include: Garry Landreth, Ross Banister, Connie Adler, Bob Abrahamson, George Woodruff, Gerald Marsh, Bill Goodin, Dick Meier, Chris Thurman, Paul Warren, States Skipper, Robert Packard, Steve Cretin, and Chris Deily.

Part 1

Recognizing Sin's Role
in Our Emotions

1

THAT HARD INWARD LOOK

In 1973 I devoured the book *Whatever Became of Sin?* by the late Karl Menninger, renowned psychiatrist and son of a Presbyterian minister. In his book he grieved over the societal trend of condoning moral weakness by calling it meaningless behavior. During decades of treating mental disorders he had observed a loosening of personal responsibility to excuse clear incidences of wrongful living.

Apparently our culture was outgrowing old-fashioned Christian ethics. "It's not my fault," the reasoning would go. "It's just that my world is changing and I have to do what is necessary to keep up." Personal soul-searching had given way to easy rationalizations.

He cited many examples of this trend. Company employees might cut corners to complete a job as easily as possible. There was an increasing tolerance of alcohol and drug abuse. Laziness in general was on the rise. Sexual promiscuity was becoming rampant. "What is this then," Dr. Menninger wrote, "other than clear, typical unadulterated sin? What else can you call it?"[1] It was refreshing for me to hear the word "sin" spoken by someone other than a salvation-preaching, red-faced minister. It was astounding at that time to know of a prominent person in the psychiatric field who used the word.

By prompting his audience to consider the core problem of sin, his goal was to hold individuals accountable before God for the behaviors that might otherwise be excused as part of a declining societal standard. "Sin must be dealt with in the private courts of the individual heart,"[2] he explained. I liked what I read because it gave me hope that those of us in the helping professions could hold to an uncompromising understanding of sin's role in human problems without buckling under the pressure to go with the flow of public opinion.

When I first read his book, I was an eager sponge, wanting to soak in ideas that would tell me about human nature and the origins of emotional pain. His bold encouragement caused me to question where sin factored into personal problems that we each face—family tension, anger, adultery, depression. I became increasingly convinced that we can indeed make great discoveries regarding environmental influences on our personal problems, but until we grapple seriously with the question of sin—*my* sin—we only gain partial understanding of the self.

"If Dad had not done that," the theory assumes, "I wouldn't be struggling as I am with anger."... Yet even if Dad had been a perfect saint, that person would still have some emotional dysfunction by virtue of indwelling sin.

In psychotherapeutic circles, beginning with Freud and extending to the present, there has been a long-standing tendency to assume that depression, anxiety, defensiveness, and the like are a direct result of wrong input from significant others, mostly our parents. This is called determinism. Thousands of volumes have been written describing how persons with improper early input are doomed to emotional duress until they successfully confront the errors of the past and learn new ways of interacting with the environment. Indeed, these theories often offer helpful insights and point the way toward improved lifestyle patterns. But they lack full credibility when they do not adequately address our spiritual disease.

Even Christian theorists can miss the mark as they explain the origins of emotional strains. Many will assert, correctly enough, that our environmental ills detract from our capacity to comprehend spiritual truths. But few extensively comment on the fact that we have a natural propensity toward emotional problems (regardless of our histories) due to indwelling sin. They leave the impression that individuals would surely thrive if only they had not experienced pain inflicted by significant others. For example, the person who experiences too much anger can be trained to see that Dad offered conditional love, thereby predisposing that person to contend excessively with others. "If Dad had not done that," the theory assumes, "I wouldn't be struggling as I am with anger."

That is only partially true. Perhaps if Dad had more properly prepared the child to respond to common frustrations, things might have been easier for that person as an adult. Yet even if Dad had been a perfect saint, that person would still have some emotional dysfunction by virtue of indwelling sin.

I addressed this issue with a woman we'll call Connie after spending several sessions getting to know her and learning of her tendencies toward depression. Slender and in her mid-forties, she was a single mother with one child out of the home and the other in high school. Her husband had abandoned her ten years prior.

"He was a runner," she told me. "He could never face problems like a man. Sometimes he would pay his child support and sometimes he wouldn't. Even though we've been apart for so long he still brings me grief because of his unreliability."

What was worse, Connie's family history was tainted. Her mother was pleasant enough, yet she was also very fragile. Not knowing how to respond to Connie's real-life problems, she would attempt to sugarcoat any frustration that might be expressed. "You just need to trust God more," she would say. This had produced years of conflict between the two because Connie hated feeling pitied. She yearned to talk freely with her mother, but realistically she knew that their relationship would always be shallow.

Connie's dad was a different story altogether. Whereas her mother was pleasant, the father was gruff. "Every now and then he might be in a good mood," she told me, "but you learn never to get your hopes up with him." As a girl she had feared him. When he became angry he could fly into a rage and give severe scoldings or beatings.

On three or four occasions in her early teens he had made sexually suggestive remarks, and though no abuse occurred she felt violated. "It's an eerie feeling," she told me, "to know that your own father could be so lewd. I hate him for his total lack of respect for me, yet I wish I felt differently."

Connie had been to other counselors who had trained her to focus on her feelings toward her parents. Through the counseling, she had developed a blaming mind-set that only seemed to fuel her emotional imbalance. Whereas in the past she had suppressed her angry feelings, she now was much more vocal in expressing her disregard for her childhood. But as she put it, "I'm more in touch with my old hidden anger, but I'm *still* depressed."

I expressed to Connie that I genuinely respected her need to sift through the deficient input received in her developmental years. And I told her that it was important to come to peace with her parents for the errors in their rearing of her. But then I added a perspective that she had not contemplated deeply. "What would you think if I suggested that making peace with your parents is only part of the solution to your depression? While you need to reevaluate the messages inherent in their treatment of you, you'll ultimately need to address a much more fundamental problem."

"I'm willing to listen," she replied. "To be honest, I've never felt fully comfortable in laying *all* the blame for my problems at their feet. What do you have in mind?"

"I'm going to suggest that you would be having difficulties even if your childhood had been wonderful. My reason for saying this is because I know you possess the sin nature. It's alive and kicking within, and it has many implications for your emotional condition.

"Most people can relate to the matter of sin," I continued, "when they think about their inability to work their way into heaven. But I'm convinced that it is at work in our lives as shown through troublesome emotions like depression or anxiety or bitterness. The stain of sin upon each of us is no small matter to be brushed aside lightly."

WHY WE'RE RELUCTANT TO DISCUSS SIN

It is not popular in psychotherapeutic circles to discuss the effects of indwelling sin on our emotions. I have pondered why many are reluctant to address this issue as an integral part of psychological healing, and I have concluded several things:

1. *The discussion of sin as related to emotional or relational problems is often reduced to simplistic legalistic jargon and pat answers.* Repeatedly I have heard people complain that they are weary of advisors who say to "give it to the Lord" when they feel inner pain. I don't blame them. Though generally well intended, many of these advisors either have no clue regarding the meaning of the emotions or they have a strong need to fit people into neat comfort zones. Legalistic advice emphasizes external correctness at the expense of ignoring real internal issues. Jesus described the legalists of His day as "whitewashed tombs," clean on the outside but dead in their real spirituality.

So let's determine that an examination of the spiritual roots to our problems will entail far more than superficial dispensing of religious dos and don'ts. Spiritual self-examination requires us to respond to questions regarding our interactive styles with both humans and God.

2. *We prefer blaming over assuming personal responsibility.* Perhaps the most troubling by-product of traditional psy-

chotherapy is the tendency to point the finger at others with the accusation "If only you hadn't . . ." Though I am sure that many counselors do not intend to encourage a blaming mind-set, that is the net result nonetheless.

Though it is unflattering to admit, virtually all of us have a lazy streak regarding personal growth. We know that healthy living requires choices irrespective of others' failures, yet we gravitate toward the tendency to blame because it gives an easy excuse for our imperfections. We say, "I know I shouldn't feel insecure, *but* my dad was so abrasive I just cringe whenever someone else rejects me."

Sin is not a friendly subject. Yet it exists.

We each possess free will. So if we continue in anger, depression, anxiety, or whatever, it is due at least in part to choice. I am not suggesting that we should never attribute pain to the input given by others. To do so would be a denial of our human interdependence. But I am suggesting that we be willing to take a hard look inside by asking, "In spite of the suffering at the hand of others, what contributions have I made to my current undesirable status?"

3. *We feel judged when someone talks to us about sin.* I recall a conversation more than fifteen years ago in which a colleague said, "I don't like talking about sin with my clients because I try to create an atmosphere of acceptance, not judgment."

I asked, "Why do you assume that the discussion of sin implies judgment?"

He responded, "Sin is negative. As soon as you mention it, people feel like you are assuming a parental role over them. I don't want a reputation of speaking to people in condescending ways."

Consider this analogy. I have had knee surgery. Suppose when I consulted the surgeon, he thought, "I see clearly what Les Carter's problem is, but I don't want to tell him about it because it is negative." If he beats around the bush and never talks with me about the trouble in my knee, he would be woefully negligent in his treatment of me.

Sin is not a friendly subject. Yet it exists. Let's discuss it, but let's also refrain from any hint of judgment. It is possible to explore the sin issue descriptively, without condescension. Just as you would expect a surgeon to talk with you about the real problems of the body, a therapist has the responsibility to discuss all elements of emotional suffering.

4. *We dislike admitting that we respond to others' sinfulness with sin.* Most people who examine the pain of the past are able to see the sinfulness that propelled another's misdeeds. For example, if a mother was too rigid or a father was emotionally unavailable, one can say, "Their walk with God was incomplete, and the result was their wrong behavior." It is usually clear when someone else exhibits a lack of spiritual balance.

But what about *our* response to that wrong input? When do we take the time out to recognize that we too have contributed in our own willful way to an unhealthy atmosphere? Too many adults who look backward at abuse or neglect ignore the reality that much of their resulting resentment or hatred or insecurity is itself sinful. We respond to sin with sin, but because our own behavior is a reaction to someone else's initiative, we overlook its seriousness. We prefer to run from the ugly truth that we too have a hand in our own demise.

By exploring the relationship between our own sinfulness and our emotional problems, we are going to encourage a mind-set anchored in the notion that "The buck stops here." If someone else has succumbed to sinful behavior, I am under no obligation to respond in kind. By developing an awareness of *my* sinfulness, I can be the one who chooses not to pass wrongful input along to the next generation.

In discussing this concept with Connie, I asked her to consider how her emotions could not always be attributed to an overbearing dad or a weak mother or a negligent husband. "Being honest, none of us has had perfection in our most important relationships. Suffering is part of the human condition. Therefore, if we were so inclined, we could always find someone to blame for the woes we currently experience. I'm curious to know, though, how you have come to choose angry or insecure responses on your own. Surely it's not always due to these other people in your life."

A slight smile crossed her face as she thought for a moment. "I feel like the kid caught with her hand in the cookie jar." Then she added, "Sometimes when I'm irritable or moody the thought flashes through my mind 'Connie, look what you're doing to yourself.' I know the difference between right and wrong. I've read books and attended lectures about the Christian walk. But in spite of my knowledge something inside blocks me from proceeding as I should."

"It would be easy to blame it on your circumstances, both past and present," I said, "but I can tell by the way you are speaking that you know you can't put all your burdens on others.

"What you just spoke," I continued, "sounds remarkably similar to Paul's lament in Romans 7 when he wrote, 'I know that nothing good lives in me, that is, in my sinful nature. For I have the desire to do what is good, but I cannot carry it out' (v. 18 NIV). He was speaking of the war we each wage with indwelling sin. Paul certainly had his share of historical problems to contend with, but he was willing to step forward and admit that he also contributed to his own demise by following his inclination toward sin."

"Does this mean that I should dismiss my past problems as insignificant?" Connie quizzed.

"Not at all. I think it can be extremely helpful to understand the learned patterns that result from your interchanges with others. Sometimes human input can be so powerful that it causes a person to become derailed from living in the optimal ways designed by God. I am saying that to properly correct your misguided patterns you need to also factor in your own inborn tendencies."

STEPS TOWARD ULTIMATE HEALING

When I work with people who, like Connie, are seeking ultimate healing, I follow a general three-fold game plan.

Step #1: Identify the emotions and behavioral patterns that are problematic. As simple as this step may sound, it is not. Many people have hidden emotions or patterns of thought that plague them, yet they have not properly learned to call a spade a spade. For instance, many people allow fear to dictate their decisions, yet they have no clue that fear is powerfully at work inside. They may assume that if they are not overly intimidated, fear is not in play. Or perhaps persons have repetitive dependency problems, but they think of themselves as highly independent. Claiming that they are able to make decisions on their own, they may remain blind to the many other ways dependency is shown.

We tend to live with blinders regarding emotional dysfunctions because of a tendency to stereotype. This identification process, which is ongoing in counseling, is crucial to ultimate healing since it causes us to develop awareness and honesty.

Step #2: Understand the root causes for problematic emotions and behaviors. It is this aspect of change that tends to be deterministic in most counseling offices. Suppose you have identified a problem with false guilt, and you realize that it causes you to act phony because you are afraid of the presumed rejection that would come if people learned of your imperfections. Part of your reason for having this emotion could be understood as a by-product of a judgmental early home atmosphere. So it would be appropriate to explore the perceived messages from significant others that led to this tendency.

But, in addition, it is necessary to question how your natural inclination toward sin played a role in this guilt. That would require an examination of human nature, irrespective of environmental influences. And it would call for an exploration of scriptural insights that might also shed light on the reasons for your guilt.

Ultimate healing requires the examination of all factors that perpetuate suffering. We need not be bound by the traditional viewpoints of determinism, which dismiss our spiritual disease as a learned inhibition. Nor do we need to cling to outmoded legalistic dogma that rejects any psychological reasoning regarding emotional pain. We can blend the two fields together (indeed, Scripture already has done it for us) and forge a well-rounded understanding of the nature of our emotional ills.

Yielding to the Holy Spirit is no simple process anchored in pat answers.

Step #3: Yield your mind to the Holy Spirit. Romans 12:2 declares that transformation occurs by the renewing of the mind. Specifically I take this to mean that we can adjust the habits and thought patterns caused by wrong environmental input and by inborn sin, choosing to commit to the thoughts of God as described in His Word. When we commit to this renewal process, the Holy Spirit becomes the guide who enables us to break from the clutches of the world and the flesh.

Yielding to the Holy Spirit is no simple process anchored in pat answers. Some might advise: "Just pray hard enough and God will heal you." But that is not sufficient. Yielding to the Holy Spirit means that we know Him. We are familiar with His directives. We are submissive to His authority. It requires that we renew our commitment to Him daily. Yielding is nothing less than giving our wills to God, acknowledging that His ways, and His alone, are sufficient to overcome the patterns established in us by the environment or by the sin nature.

Yielding our minds to God is more than memorizing His rules and living accordingly. It means that we have laid down our claims to self-rule and have invited Christ to live in us for

God's glory. It is this willingness that gives committed Christians a distinct advantage in the effort to remedy inner tensions.

In the next several chapters we will explore a model that will explain how sin has given us a predisposition toward emotional duress and how the environment can feed the problems produced by sin. My goal is to encourage you, the reader, to break away from the bondage implied by determinism. As you see that emotional problems are ultimately caused by mankind's collective fall into sin, you can conclude that ultimate healing occurs when we right ourselves, not with inappropriate humans, but with God Himself.

Notes

1. Karl Menninger, *Whatever Became of Sin?* (New York: Hawthorn, 1973), 158.
2. Ibid., 180.

2

THE ORIGIN OF EMOTIONAL STRUGGLES

As I spoke with Connie about the effects of sin on her depression, I asked her to consider what really occurred on that day when Adam's life was changed in the Garden of Eden. "I'm sure you are familiar with the story of Adam and Eve," I said, "but I wonder if you've contemplated the meaning of it."

"Not really. I guess I've just thought that they got into a bunch of bad apples."

I smiled. "Don't worry, for years it never occurred to me that Adam's story had much to do with my life. But I've come to realize that he represents you and me. The Bible teaches that Adam's problems put into motion the patterns of personal pain just as Christ's victories put into motion the possibility of living life in an abundant way. First Corinthians 15:22 says that *in Adam* all die. This tells us that an understanding of all human tragedy begins with a knowledge of what it means to be 'in Adam.'

"Try to imagine, if you can, what life must have been like for Adam and Eve prior to the fall into sin. It would be fun just to think of a life that knew no problems."

"I've never really thought about it," she replied, "but I guess they had it great, didn't they. Wow, just think of a life with no arguments or criticism or insecurity. I guess that is why we call Eden a paradise."

"We don't know how long they lived before the advent of sin," I mentioned. "But we can surmise that they had open communion with God and very pleasant interchanges with each other. I try to imagine if they ever disagreed prior to sin, and I've concluded that, if they did, it was because they were trying to out-please each other!" We both chuckled at the thought.

"If you read Genesis 3 carefully," I continued, "you'll notice that Satan was able to lure them out of this wonderful state, and when he did all manner of emotional problems were set into motion."

In the Genesis account of mankind's fall into sin, we see a snowball effect. One emotional problem led to another, then another, then another. Keep in mind that the story of Adam and Eve is the story of you and me. What they experienced is representative of what we experience. Although their situation occurred thousands of years ago, human nature is still the same. As we understand the problems that came upon them, we lay a foundation that will help us understand our own negative propensities.

THE FIVE BASIC EMOTIONAL STRUGGLES

When Adam and Eve chose to defy God they immediately experienced five major emotional problems: pride, fear, loneliness, inferiority, and anger. Though we may currently struggle with innumerable negative emotions, all can be understood as derivatives of these five.

PRIDE

Just as I encouraged Connie to imagine life prior to sin, you too may try to picture life in those days. Communication between Adam and Eve was quite satisfactory. Their minds were not cluttered with thoughts of lust or envy, but instead they were pure. Empathy was present in their interactions as they illustrated an understanding of one another's feelings and needs. Surely they experienced ongoing joy. Laughter came easily. Contentment and peace were felt in abundance. Their relationship with God must have been full since Scripture implies that they were able to audibly communicate with Him.

We could use the word *proud* to summarize the way Adam and Eve felt about themselves. By that I mean that they felt a deep and abiding sense of pleasure and satisfaction with the life God had given them. God had desired that they experience His joy, and they did. Today we continue to use the word *pride* in a positive way. We say, "Take pride in your country," or, "Be proud of your children." Such an emotion implies that we can maintain a positive regard for who we are and about life in general.

In his effort to gain dominion over Adam and Eve, Satan chose to attack this positive aspect of pride. Isaiah 14:12–14 describes how he himself had already succumbed to the other kind of pride. His goal in the garden was to entice Adam to endorse the mind-set already in him. He appealed first to Eve's pride and then Adam's, creating a desire for self-worship by drawing them away from God and into themselves. Sinful pride is clearly the first and foremost of all emotional problems. God's gift of a paradise existence became twisted:

> Now the serpent was more crafty than any beast of the field which the Lord God had made. And he said to the woman, "Indeed, has God said, 'You shall not eat from any tree of the garden'?" And the woman said to the serpent, "From the fruit of the trees of the garden we may eat; but from the fruit of the tree which is in the middle of the garden, God has said, 'You shall not eat from it or touch it, lest you die.'" And the serpent said to the woman, "You surely shall not die! For God knows that in the day you eat from it your eyes will be opened, and you will be like God, knowing good and evil." (Genesis 3:1–5)

Prior to their conversation, Eve was without blemish. She had a high sense of importance and self-esteem. Recall a time in your own life when you had an extra bounce in your gait, hummed an upbeat tune, or reached out to another person with a friendly hello and a warm pat on the back. At such times, you know an inward glow as you think, *All is well. I'm pleased with life.* Now imagine how it would be to feel that way every hour of the day, every day of the week. That's what life was like for Eve. She didn't just have a taste of the good life. She personified it!

Sinful pride ... is at the center of all other troublesome emotions.

Satan always looks for ways to gain an advantage, even when the odds seem unrealistically stacked against him. He thought, *I'll try to get Eve to feel dissatisfied about who she is and what she has with God. I'll tempt her to crave an even greater sense of self-importance than she has now.* So he threw out the bait, in effect saying, "Eve, how would you like to be like God? How would you like to make yourself the center of the universe? If you think life is grand now, just imagine how good it could be if you called all the shots."

In essence, Satan's temptation caused Eve to carry her desire for satisfaction with life to the extreme, becoming completely absorbed with her own thoughts about how life ought to proceed. That's what sinful pride does. In the original instruction to refrain from the Tree of the Knowledge of Good and Evil, God was in effect communicating, "I'm the only one with the ultimate knowledge of right and wrong. Do not attempt to outsmart Me. Instead, live in submission to My ways." By eating of this tree, Eve (and, shortly afterward, Adam) was communicating, "I'm really quite wise in my own right. *I'd* rather have the ultimate say regarding right and wrong."

Sinful pride is defined as a preoccupation with self's needs, desires, and importance. It represents an overindulgence of self. It is the craving to be in control. As such, it puts humans at odds with God since it represents direct defiance against His exalted order.

With Adam and Eve's fateful decision to put self first, sinful pride became central to human nature. The positive feeling of pride turned into selfish desire, and, once germinated, Adam and Eve were unable to dislodge it from their personalities. You might say they became addicted to it. Being representatives of all subsequent humanity, their struggle has been passed along generational lines to the present day.

Furthermore, since sinful pride is the original emotion of mankind's Fall, we can surmise that it is at the center of all other troublesome emotions. Whether an individual is prone to overt emotional displays (such as shouting or whining) or covert emotional expressions (such as holding grudges or withdrawal), pride is at the base. Examine a broad array of emotions and you will find that resentment, arrogance, hostile anger, envy, jealousy, ultrasensitivity, defensiveness, insecurity, false guilt, infatuation, depression, and even loneliness all have pride at their core. An understanding of any other emotion would be incomplete without an understanding of pride.

Now consider something else. You are guaranteed to experience sinful pride regardless of your background experiences. Clearly if you were unloved or abused, you would easily succumb to self-preoccupied feelings. But even if you were warmly nurtured or encouraged, you would still have the struggle. That is part of what it means to be born into sin. You are "in Adam."

Consider selfishness in very young children. Before a child has a chance to learn self-preoccupied thinking, this trait appears. When playing with other children, a fourteen-month-old baby is concerned with "me." Sharing must be taught and reinforced. Grabbing and whining are behaviors no one has ever had to teach a child. They are innate.

As a child progresses through elementary, junior high, and high school, selfish tendencies remain. Fueled by competitiveness, a need for approval, and a desire for status, sinful pride remains firmly entrenched. The only difference between one individual and the next is the means by which the pride is manifested. It becomes the task of each one, then, to come to terms with his own pride, recognizing the influence it has on his life.

Perhaps the best way to determine the extent of fear in your life is to check your level of defensiveness.

When we harbor sinful pride, it is likely to be evidenced in many everyday behaviors:

- When someone is argumentative you think, *How dare he disagree with me!*
- In a family discussion your input is not immediately understood, so you press your point more powerfully.
- In social conversations you interrupt another person because he is too slow to make his point.
- Critical thoughts come too easily as you relate with family members.
- You secretly wish others could handle problems with the same common sense that guides you.
- You have a list of expectations others should meet before you act genuinely accepting of them.
- Maintaining a proper public image can be all-important, even if it requires cover-up or evasiveness.

These illustrations barely scratch the surface of pride's manifestations. You will be one step closer to understanding your sin nature when you can admit the multitudinous ways self-preoccupation occurs. Most of us are guilty of stereotyping when we think of the term *pride,* assuming that it merely implies haughtiness or conceit. But these examples show it to be an extremely broad trait found in any relational circumstance.

FEAR

After sinful pride became lodged in Adam's personality, fear was the next troublesome emotion to surface. As the first husband and wife defied God, their eyes were opened to the severity of their decision:

> And they heard the sound of the Lord God walking in the garden in the cool of the day, and the man and his wife hid themselves from the presence of the Lord God among the trees of the garden. . . . And [the man] said, "I heard the sound of Thee in the Garden, and I was afraid because I was naked; so I hid myself." (Genesis 3:8, 10)

Adam and Eve experienced a startling turn of events. Having indulged their desire for self-importance, they soon realized that they were not equipped to handle their new position, and panic struck. Their decision had not been a good one; they were unable to fulfill the task of being a god. As they felt the initial repercussions of their inability to function without God's guidance, apprehension overwhelmed them.

Today we have the same propensity toward fear. Because we are sinners who through pride have made wrong decisions, we are each prone toward doubt and dread. No one is exempt, even those who seem self-reliant. This sense of fear may be obvious to one who is indecisive, doubtful, or prone to phobias. Or it may be more subtle in one who is rigid, cautious, or phony.

Perhaps the best way to determine the extent of fear in your life is to check your level of defensiveness. Just as fear caused an immediate act of cover-up in Adam and Eve, we too illustrate this emotion by the way we guard ourselves from being known. We rationalize our decisions. We refuse to admit weaknesses. We offer excuses for our mistakes. We shift the focus onto others to avoid taking the rap ourselves. At first glance, we may not see the fear in these behaviors since they can be cloaked in anger or aloofness or seeming indifference.

Yet close examination shows that the defensive person is insecure and uncertain about his real value.

The level of fear in our lives is proportional to the level of
sinful pride. The more self-absorbed we are, the more appre-
hensive we are about the approval or rejection of others. Undue
fear reveals the prideful need to be in a god-like position of
control, "calling the shots" according to self's dictates. So even
though you may not fit the stereotypical image of a fearful person, your self-preoccupied lifestyle indicates how powerfully
this emotion plays a role in your interactions.

For example, a man who feels a need to be treated with
dignity and respect may tell himself that he *must* be given special treatment by his wife when he arrives home from work. If
his wife is not in the best of moods when he gets home, a type
of fear appears. On the surface he may exhibit irritability, but
beneath the surface he is thinking, *Oh no, she's not treating me
in the grand fashion I had hoped for. I can't handle it. What will
I do?* The fear may be so subtle that he does not identify it;
nonetheless, it is there and at work.

To further understand our natural inclination toward fear,
consider some experiences common to children (who illustrate
raw human nature). Children can be frightened by such things
as a loud noise, a harsh rebuke, a new circumstance, or a dark
room. As children grow older the blatant fears begin to subside,
but something remains. They become conscientious about social status, appearance, evaluations, and the like. Then, as they
develop a more adult mind-set, their fears become more abstract as they dread rejections, loss of status, financial uncertainty, or condescending communications. Like pride, fear is a
natural and predictable emotion. It is part of being "in Adam."
The only difference between one person and the next is the
substance and degree of that fear.

Once we recognize the presence of fear in us, we can
gain insight into the meaning of common behavior.

✔ You are careful not to reveal flaws. This might cause you to
   seem weak or unlikable.

- When someone confronts you, you are thinking of a rebuttal.
- There is a lack of spontaneity in your life. You prefer to keep things predictable.
- You feel insecure as you realize that you do not compare favorably with someone else.
- The possibility of being rejected is unsettling. You are obsessed with why someone doesn't like you.

Do you see the snowball effect beginning? First, mankind was enticed into thinking more highly about self than was warranted, elevating self to the position reserved for God. The result was a warped sinful pride. Then, because people were not created to be gods, fear gained a foothold as mankind tried to become reconciled to an imbalanced life position. That fear lead to the next of the five basic emotional problems—loneliness.

LONELINESS

Once mankind fell into indulgent pride, leading to fear and insecurity, a third problem developed—the problem of loneliness. Simply defined, *loneliness* is a feeling of separation, emptiness, and isolation from God and others. It can even be felt in a sense of estrangement from oneself, as in the case of the person who says, "I'm not even sure I know myself."

We think of a lonely person as one with few acquaintances or as very retiring. . . .This emotion is not that one-dimensional.

Scripture describes what happened once Adam and Eve hid from God in fear: "Then the Lord God called to the man, and said to him, 'Where are you?'" (Genesis 3:9).

The perfect fellowship Adam and Eve experienced with God was broken. We cannot be sure that Adam and Eve could see God physically or converse with Him audibly, though the implication is that they enjoyed an open line of communication with Him. But we do know that, once sin entered their lives, communication with God was lost.

Not only were Adam and Eve separated from God, they were irreversibly separated from each other. They no longer felt the desire or the ability to be fully open. Deception had replaced their perfect trust. Their understanding for each other was lost, their communication more calculated. Even though they were to remain together as partners, their relationship had taken a giant step downward. They faced the feelings of aloneness and isolation that God never desired for them to experience.

Adam and Eve's unhappy plight has been passed along to the successive generations. Every person has felt the pain of loneliness. Each of us has experienced the feeling of being disconnected from others. We have each yearned to be touched more intimately, to be comprehended more completely, to be loved more fully. No one is immune.

Many overlook the reality of loneliness in their lives because of the tendency to stereotype. We think of a lonely person as one with few acquaintances or as very retiring. And whereas those traits may be common to some who are lonely, this emotion is not that one-dimensional. Loneliness can be felt by the socially active person who nonetheless feels that others cannot be trusted with delicate matters of deep concern. It is experienced by the person lusting to be sexually connected with an ideal-other. It is felt by the one who feels unduly criticized. It is experienced when one's career has a setback. Loneliness is felt when our children choose not to obey. It is at the core of the person who has a "chip on his shoulder" and proclaims a need for no one. And it is a motivating force in the feeling of infatuation.

We have each yearned for more significant interaction and understanding between ourselves and our loved ones. Honesty requires us to admit that our relationships never achieve perfect unity. In marriage relations we have communi-

cation gaps and personality differences. In parent-child communication it is called the generation gap. At work we may
sense an adversarial relationship between management and
subordinates. All this represents loneliness.

To illustrate how loneliness is part of being "in Adam,"
think about the earliest times we felt this emotion. Even young
infants struggle with loneliness; they cry when a parent puts
them to bed. They reach out in the hope of being held. This is
not a trained reaction. It is indigenous to who they are. No child
enters life feeling perfectly connected with all significant others. That is because of the sin nature.

Notice how this emotion impacts you through your adult
years:

- You complain about the lack of warmth in your most impor-
  tant relationships.
- Sexual themes or cravings for intimacy recur in your thought
  patterns. You yearn for deeper love.
- You become uncomfortable when you do not naturally know
  what to say to someone else, whether it is in a social situa-
  tion or a serious conversation.
- Sadness or emptiness is part of your life. You struggle with
  "Who am I?" questions.
- Something seems missing in your closest relations.

The way you are treated by others will either increase or decrease the intensity of this emotion, yet you are prone to it regardless of the circumstances.

INFERIORITY

As Adam and Eve began to feel the repercussions of their
decision to defy God in sinful pride, they not only felt fear and
loneliness but lost their high position in the home God had giv-
en them. Whereas God's original plan was to give them a glorious life that included a continual relationship of joy with Him,

the onset of sin drove them out of their paradise as God imposed upon them the consequences of their decision. This created the emotional struggle with inferiority.

Inferiority struggles are
revealed in a wide array of
behaviors and associated emotions.

Beginning in Genesis 3:11, we read about the discussion God had with the serpent, Eve, and Adam. In the scriptural account, God does most of the talking as He explains the inevitable struggle that will result because of their separation from Him. Each will experience a lowered order of living. Genesis 3:23–24 summarizes this judgment: "Therefore the Lord God sent him out from the garden of Eden, to cultivate the ground from which he was taken. So He drove the man out."

Symbolically, by letting Adam struggle with the consequence of attempting to be his own master, God was saying, "I'm going to let you experience just how incapable you are of running your own ship, then perhaps you will understand your need for Me more clearly." As a result, each of us, being of Adam's seed, has an instinctive understanding that we do not fully possess the ability to be what God wants us to be. Deep down we know we are inadequate to face all the challenges life offers. Romans 1:20 reiterates that message by saying that God has revealed to every person a knowledge of His divine majesty, and we all at some level (conscious or subconscious) know that we are not perfect as He is. God wants us to recognize our inferiority so that we will respond to His invitation to restored fellowship with Him through Christ Jesus.

Inferiority struggles are revealed in a wide array of behaviors and associated emotions. Some individuals, overwhelmed by their sense of inadequacy, develop a cowering, timid nature and assume that they must be resigned to an inferior position. These people are too willing to admit guilt. They have difficulty accepting forgiveness. They push themselves to perform well in order to warrant love. Often they struggle with the fallout from being nonassertive.

At the other extreme, some respond to their feelings of inferiority by seeking to make themselves feel superior. These people assume that, if they gain a competitive edge on someone else (*anyone* else), they will rid themselves of the feeling of unworthiness. Consequently they go to great lengths to gain the upper hand. They may become overachievers, critics, manipulators, braggarts, snobs. They may give unsolicited advice freely. They feel it necessary to rebut someone who makes errant statements. But these behaviors do nothing to solve the feelings of inferiority. The striving for superiority only provides a temporary satisfaction. Inferiority is not truly resolved by putting others down.

The important truth to remember is that we are inferior to Adam's original position of sinlessness, but no human is inferior to another. Mankind's basic inferiority is a consequence of broken fellowship with God. We are each equally guilty of sin (just as we are equally loved by Him). Our resolution to inferiority, therefore, does not rest in our competitive standing with others, but in a restored relationship with God.

When does this struggle with inferiority begin? When young children explore the world around them (getting into cabinets, playing with forbidden objects, and so on), they soon realize that they are capable of eliciting displeasure from adults. They easily feel guilty or frightened or insecure. Their feeling is not entirely given to them by others; it arises from within. It is natural to the child, part of being "in Adam." And as they grow they become increasingly aware, often painfully so, that they are unable to perform the same deeds as Mom and Dad. They must lean on adults to teach them to speak, to drive them to school, to tell them when to go to bed and when to get up. Even in the most loving homes, the child perceives the message, "You are not fully adequate."

As the years pass, some children learn to put that inadequacy into proper perspective by minimizing comparisons. Yet there still remains the nagging question, "Am I *really* OK?" For instance, in adulthood we still are tempted to cover our weaknesses and accentuate the positive so that we appear to be on top. And we still struggle to win favor and to gain an edge over others to keep from being on the bottom of the social heap. As long as we are in our earthly bodies, we will continue to question self-worth.

Common experiences that indicate this inferiority struggle include:

- You sometimes apologize for things that really require no apology.
- You will compensate for your weaknesses by proving how good you are in one of your skills.
- Perfectionism is your way of trying to rid your world of nagging imperfections.
- Even when you have received forgiveness, you can still cling to guilt.
- When someone tells you an interesting story, you try to one-up it with a better story.

Your struggle in the inferior-superior realm may indeed be exacerbated by family and social experiences, yet they are ultimately experienced because of the flaws brought on by indwelling sin.

ANGER

The final basic emotion Adam and Eve experienced as they were driven out of the Garden was anger. Adam and Eve did not take their fall in stride. They harbored feelings of resentment. Going from paradise to a life of toil was not easy to accept, leaving them with great frustration. You can imagine that though they had no arguments prior to the Fall that was not true in the aftermath. I can easily picture Adam grumbling at his wife as they hurried away from their home. He probably had a few choice words for her about her vulnerability to the serpent. But she probably did not idly receive those words. She too must have been agitated as she complained about the lack of leadership he had portrayed.

We stereotypically think of anger as shouting or slamming doors or hurling insults. But it is far more than that.

As they bore children, their offspring inherited the same emotional problems, and they too were easily disposed to anger. That is vividly evidenced in Cain's feelings toward his brother, Abel:

> And Abel, on his part also brought the firstlings of his flock and of their fat portions. And the Lord had regard for Abel and for his offering; but for Cain and for his offering He had no regard. So Cain became very angry and his countenance fell. . . . And it came about when they were in the field, that Cain rose up against Abel his brother and killed him. (Genesis 4:4–5, 8)

Finding themselves in the unwanted position of lowered status, Adam and Eve became dissatisfied. That dissatisfaction led to the emotion that primarily advocates self's needs and desires—anger. Notice that the individual who expresses anger is basically conveying a sense of self-preservation. It may be that someone has rejected you or ignored you or spoken harshly to you. Your anger prompts you to think, *Hey, don't treat me that way! How about some dignity and respect?* But because our fallenness prompts us to think selfishly, that anger can be managed in a wide variety of unhealthy choices.

No one is immune to anger. Many times in my counseling practice I have heard people claim that they do not experience anger. But that is not so. We stereotypically think of anger as shouting or slamming doors or hurling insults. But it is far more than that. Anger includes those moments when we are unduly critical, sarcastic, bossy, or punitively silent. When we say we feel frustrated or agitated or annoyed or tense, we are invariably referring to our anger—it is that broad in its expressions. Because we each have known experiences in which we felt mistreated, misunderstood, spoken down to, or ignored, we have each felt anger. And because we are all sinners, we will naturally handle this emotion inappropriately.

As with Cain's anger, our anger is usually misguided by our absorption with self. Though most of us have not gone as far in expressing anger as Cain did, Jesus Christ made clear that we have the capacity to do so. In Matthew 5:21–22 Jesus indicates that our feelings of angry hate are on a par with the act of murder. That is, though we may never have killed anyone, we can be pushed to think about it.

To be reminded how this anger is part of our inborn sin nature, consider the earliest times a child will feel this way. As young children first consciously interact with people they display anger. They become heated when we do not meet their perceived needs or desires in the fashion they deem correct. So they scream. As these kids grow older they might be more sophisticated in expressing the anger, yet frustrations and annoyances are registered virtually every day. It is inherent in each personality.

An awareness of this emotion will help you identify anger in many common circumstances:

- Impatience is too common as you interact with your world.
- Minor problems create frustration that does not go away easily.
- Though you know it is good to forgive, that is something you struggle with.
- You seem to be on a constant search to have something better than you already possess. This represents envy.
- Depression and discouragement come over you.
- You aggravate others by a tendency to withdraw or sulk when tensions arise.

Let's keep in mind that there are some moments when anger is appropriate, when convictions and boundaries need to be upheld. But, because of our sinfulness, we have a bent toward the unhealthy rather than the healthy expressions of anger.

THE INTERACTIONS OF OUR EMOTIONS

In counseling Connie I explained how many of her emotional highs and lows were inevitable because of her sin nature. "I can appreciate how your disappointments in several close relationships have increased your emotional discomfort. But perhaps you can see that your innate feelings are more than just a reaction to people. Those feelings also represent your imperfect spiritual status."

Connie confessed, "I've always resented people who have suggested that we should just give our emotional lives to God because I've felt they were dismissing altogether the problems caused by environmental strains. These people seemed too simplistic and legalistic. Yet you are suggesting that I can incorporate both an awareness of my environment and my sin nature as I try to make sense of myself."

"That's right, and we will eventually look at how your exposure to wrong treatment feeds into the emotions you feel. But for now, by saying that emotional problems are a part of your sinfulness, I am strongly suggesting that you will need to take responsibility before God for their direction."

"I like this approach," she replied, "because it implies that I can still gain insight into myself by examining the experiences I've been through, yet ultimately I am responsible to God to make choices in the direction of my emotions."

"There is one further thing I'd like to point out before we go further," I said. "I want you to see that the five major emotions produced by sin each influences the others. They are intricately linked to one another."

Figure 2-1 identifies the five basic emotional struggles and shows that each emotion progresses into the next. From one end, we see that pride leads to fear, which feeds loneliness, which increases inferiority, which prompts anger. Or from

THE FIVE BASIC EMOTIONS

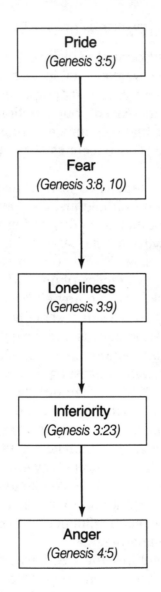

Figure 2-1

another perspective we see that anger contains elements of inferiority, loneliness, fear, and pride. Each emotion is intricately linked to the others in a cause-and-effect relationship.

In Figure 2-2, you will notice that many other emotional struggles are related to the five basic emotions. (This depiction of emotions is not exhaustive; many more could be included.) You will see again that sinful pride, being the most basic emotional problem, fuels the others. Next to each of the four remaining emotions are listed feelings or traits most closely related to them.

For example, on the fear level, we see doubt and dread. In addition, fear fosters defensiveness and phoniness. To understand the presence of these qualities in your life, you can recognize that each in their own way imply that fear is driving you at that moment.

Loneliness, with its inherent feelings of emptiness and isolation, creates a yearning for love, attention, and comfort. That yearning, if not properly resolved, can cause vulnerability to infatuations and lust. Any time a person struggles with sexual temptations, it represents a form of loneliness. In addition, loneliness can be shown in a feeling of lamentation, a sadness that bemoans a life that does not offer the rewards we would like to enjoy. That sadness can then produce grief, a feeling of emptiness due to a loss of something desired and treasured.

The struggle with inferiority also has varied manifestations, one of which is guilt. *Guilt* can be defined as a feeling of blameworthiness due to offenses committed (real or imagined). Guilt holds a person in a position of low self-esteem, causing him to feel comparatively less valuable than others. This feeling can then produce shyness as the individual stays away from experiences that might expose inadequacies. In addition, inferiority can be shown through feelings of unworthiness, usually due to messages of rejection received by others. As that feeling simmers, it can produce despair and helplessness.

The struggle with anger probably has the widest array of manifestations. As mentioned, it is expressed through many behaviors beyond the loud, shouting style of communicating. Figure 2-2 shows that it can be evidenced through feelings of resentment. That would also include struggles with hate or bitterness or even hurt. Left unresolved, depression—a sad and irritated dejection—can result. Likewise, anger can prompt a feeling of impatience when our desires are not quickly met. This emotion can then turn into worry, which has elements of both anger and fear. And this ongoing tension may either overtly or subtly contribute to problems with envy or jealousy.

The major message to be derived from Figure 2-2 is that each of the five major emotions can be manifested in different ways and that none of the emotions we experience are felt in isolation from the other.

Let's look at Connie's situation. The original problem that prompted her to call my office was depression due to feelings of rejection from her parents and her ex-husband. This tension was evidenced by her frequent episodes of anger. She did not explode every time she felt anger. Sometimes she would fret or gripe or criticize or grumble. This caused her to experience many other "cousins" of anger, such as impatience, resentment, frustration, and envy.

For Connie to understand her anger, she needed to realize how it was fed by struggles with inferiority. The ongoing anger told me that she felt lowly too often. Perhaps she was easily susceptible to guilt trips imposed by others or by messages of unworthiness.

In addition, her anger had elements of loneliness. She felt isolated, disconnected. Three very important people in her life (her former husband, her parents) were emotionally disconnected from her.

Beneath her loneliness and inferiority was unresolved fear. Though her anger may have masked fear's presence, her tension communicated, "I can't handle this! What am I going to do? What will become of me?" This explained why her anger was commonly accomplished by defensiveness and excessive rationalization.

THE INTERACTION OF EMOTIONS

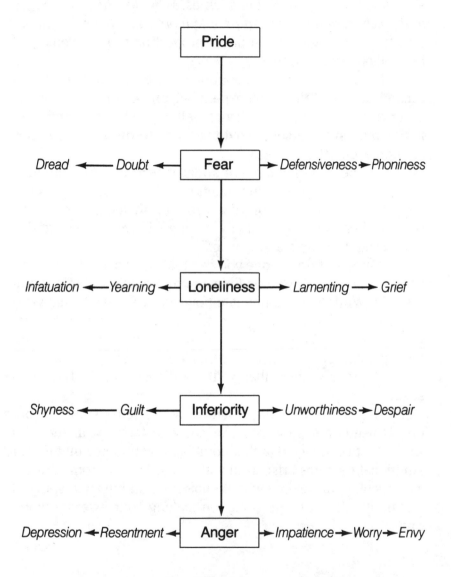

Figure 2-2

Then, finally, Connie needed to realize how pride was present in her anger. At the moment of her deepest frustration, she would indulge thoughts such as, *Why do I have to put up with such treatment? I wish people would act as I say!* The intensity of her anger was in direct proportion to the intensity of her self-preoccupation.

I spoke with Connie about how her emotions were so intricately linked. "When you experience one emotion, invariably other emotions come into play as well. If you want to thoroughly comprehend yourself, you'll take time to discover how they feed on each other."

"I'd never really thought about it before," she admitted. "For example, if you hadn't mentioned it, I would never have identified loneliness as playing a role in my feelings of anger. But now I can clearly see that I am angry because I feel so disconnected. It really makes sense."

"Another thing I hope you can realize," I said, "is that you cannot totally lay the blame for your emotional problems at others' feet. While I can appreciate how you have needs that were not addressed well, I'm going to make the assumption that you'd have emotional ups and downs even if you had fewer disappointments in your past. It's all part of being 'in Adam.'"

"Does that mean that we'll not discuss any historical issues?"

"Not at all. In future sessions we'll discuss some of your unmet needs and how you can come to terms with them," I said. "My primary goal at this point is for you to see that if your emotional tensions arise from within, rather than from your environment, your healing will ultimately be an internal, spiritual matter. It will not hinge solely on making your external world right."

3

RESOLUTIONS TO EMOTIONAL STRUGGLES

Each day we are guided by various signals and warnings, many so common we are hardly aware of them. For example, most of us begin each day with the buzzing of an alarm clock exhorting us to wake up. Our subconscious messages tell us to be cautious as we step onto the wet porcelain of the shower. Traffic signals tell us when to stop and when to go. Signs tell us how fast to travel and when to yield. At work a colaborer may give a knowing look that says, "Beware, the boss is in a bad mood."

We learn to read the faces of loved ones. We know the signals that mean all is well. We learn the ones that prompt us to be silent. Our bodies send signals alerting us to special needs. A yawn signals the need for sleep. A painful bruise tells us to treat that part of the body more tenderly. Warnings such as these are a vital part of life, giving order in what might otherwise be a chaotic world.

In the same way, our *emotions* are warning signals meant to bring order to life. In the last chapter we examined how everyone has a natural inclination toward emotional struggles and that each of those struggles is an indicator of indwelling sin. Emotions are surface symptoms that indicate a need to confront the deeper issues related to our fallen nature. As we learn to view our troublesome emotions as God's warning system, we can make adjustments to our thoughts and behaviors that put us more in line for the healthy way of life He desires for us.

In the last chapter we identified the five basic emotional struggles, and we noted how all other emotional difficulties could be understood in relation to them. As we examined those emotions separately, we noticed that each one tells us something about our ongoing struggle with human imperfection. As we learn to identify our emotions carefully, a heightened awareness unfolds. Awareness is being alert to and knowledgeable of our deepest personal needs and thoughts. Awareness is a vital first step on the road to ultimate healing. But what do we do once we become aware of our most basic emotions?

Scott came to my office seeking help for a variety of emotional strains. On the outside, most would judge him to be a normally adjusted man. He was thirty-eight, and, in spite of a few streaks of gray hair, he looked young and fit. He held a good job as an accountant with a medium-sized computer company. He was married and the father of two preadolescent girls. Though his marriage was not perfect, it was rewarding a fair amount of the time.

In our initial interview he told me of lifelong feelings of inferiority that fueled other emotions such as guilt, unworthiness, passive anger, impatience, and occasional depression. He had sought counseling elsewhere but without satisfactory results. Scott told me, "I've been told what my problems are, so I'm not lacking in my knowledge of what needs to be changed. And I've been told what I should do differently. But something's still missing. I don't feel like I'm working with the right tools."

Scott's experience is not unlike that of many others who have recurring emotional struggles. He knew what his problems were, and he even knew what some of the answers were, but he was missing the key ingredient. He still needed to discover what his emotions communicated about his imperfect spiritual condition. He needed to learn how to scour biblical truths and integrate new and lasting principles into his mental processes. As he learned to set aside the thoughts that fueled his negative emotions in favor of the timeless truth of God's Word, he could make the desirable adjustments in his life.

As we examine the antidotes to the five basic emotions produced by sin, which are presented in progressive order (as in chapter 2), it is important not to appear simplistic. I am painfully aware of how easy it is to portray truth by saying, "Just do this, and all will be well." It's not that easy. Adjusting from a life of emotional distress to personal healing is no quick process. In fact, it will require effort for the rest of our lives. Yet, as we incorporate the timeless truths of Scripture and yield to the guidance of the Holy Spirit, we can be assured that in spite of the unnaturalness of it all our growth curve can be upward.

OVERCOMING EMOTIONAL STRUGGLES

HUMILITY

In the last chapter we noted that mankind's fall into emotional turmoil originated with sinful pride. When Adam and Eve chose to elevate themselves as God, they were left with a human nature preoccupied with the importance of self, craving control. This self-absorption is indigenous to each human and is the beginning of all emotional problems.

It would stand to reason, then, that we should discover pride's opposite and build upon it as the foundation for emotional well-being. Scripture teaches that God's preference is a humble spirit rather than pride:

> God is opposed to the proud, but gives grace to the humble. (James 4:6; 1 Peter 5:5)

> Humble yourselves, therefore, under the mighty hand of God, that He may exalt you at the proper time. (1 Peter 5:6)

> And what does the Lord require of you but to do justice, to love kindness, and to walk humbly with your God? (Micah 6:8)

TURNING PRIDE INTO HUMILITY

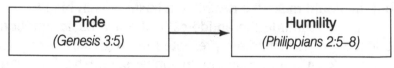

| Pride
(Genesis 3:5) | Humility
(Philippians 2:5–8) |

Figure 3-1

Philippians 2:5–8 describes a life of complete surrender to God. It explains how we can be committed to unity and servitude to others, not in a manner that makes us a doormat but in a way that enables us to show God's strength. Notice how Christ is contrasted to mankind in the Adamic state:

> Have this attitude in yourselves which was also in Christ Jesus, who, although He existed in the form of God, did not regard equality with God a thing to be grasped, but emptied Himself, taking the form of a bond-servant, and being made in the likeness of men. And being found in appearance as a man, He humbled Himself by becoming obedient to the point of death, even death on a cross. (Philippians 2:5–8)

Christ, although He could have exercised His right to be coequal with God, chose to humble Himself by taking the form of a bondslave—a freeman choosing to submit His will to the master. This was the precise opposite of Adam's mind-set. Whereas Adam became consumed with himself, Christ relinquished control. Adam catered to his preferences and desires, whereas Christ was pleased to follow God's desires.

In choosing humility, Jesus demonstrated His faith in God's ability to uphold Him in every area of need. Though Jesus experienced scorn and anguish as a result of His decision to set aside self, He also embodied love. In the end, God exalted Him, giving Him the ultimate position of glory.

Humility is defined as a lack of self-preoccupation and a modest appraisal of oneself. It is also a recognition of reasonable limits. It is a person's admission that the world is not obliged to meet personal preferences, regardless of how desirable that might seem. Although we, like Christ, will experience strains when we choose to set aside self-preoccupations, God will ultimately bless and exalt us. When we allow His nature to indwell us, we can be assured that whatever our circumstances may be, we will be given godly composure and confidence.

To acquire the mind of humility,
we must commit to nothing
short of death to self.

It is unnatural for any of us to set aside self in favor of God's leading. From the earliest days of childhood we have desired our own way. Sin has a strong influence over us and will not leave us alone. That may explain why Christ said, "If anyone wishes to come after Me, let him deny himself, and take up his cross daily, and follow Me" (Luke 9:23). To live a life pleasing to God, we must begin each day with a new decision to follow Him. If we are not choosing humility on a day-by-day basis, we will naturally lapse into the pride of life.

To acquire the mind of humility, we must commit to nothing short of death to self. Paradoxically, emotional aliveness begins when we accept the death sentence imposed on us through sin:

> Consider yourselves to be dead to sin, but alive to God in Christ Jesus. (Romans 6:11)

> The love of Christ controls us, having concluded this, that one died for all, therefore all died. (2 Corinthians 5:14)

> Set your mind on the things above, not on the things that are on earth. For you have died and your life is hidden with Christ in God. (Colossians 3:2–3)

> But God, being rich in mercy, because of His great love with which He loved us, even when we were dead in our transgressions, made us alive together with Christ (by grace you have been saved). (Ephesians 2:4–5)

The only way to find ultimate purpose and contentment in life is to consider self's preoccupations dead and to give the direction of our lives to God. That action is summarized the word *selflessness*. To be selfless means to let go of the desire to control your world in accordance with self-understanding, choosing instead to acknowledge God's control. Galatians 2:20 vividly captures the concept of selflessness: "I have been crucified with Christ; and it is no longer I who live, but Christ lives in me."

When the apostle Paul (who wrote Galatians 2:20) considered the cross, he did not think of it as only an event that covered the payment for the world's sin. He also personalized its meaning. He acknowledged that the death of Christ was a substitution for his own death. This brought him to the point of humility as he then recognized that he had no right to order the world according to his own dictates. All life was to be lived in subjection to the one who gave him a new lease on life. In Christ, he was not his own man.

I have spoken with countless individuals who have genuinely committed to Christianity but who have made virtually no link between that commitment and emotional well-being. If Christianity is to be real, it is crucial that we plug it into every emotional or relational problem. That means we will be willing to ponder the many ways we can exchange prideful thoughts for humility. We will be vigilant from the smallest emotional strains to the greatest. Examples abound:

- When disagreements arise at home, rather than complaining that you shouldn't have to struggle so, you can humbly acknowledge that misunderstandings are an inevitable part of an imperfect world.

- You can speak your opinions with confidence, yet you are not surprised or insulted when others do not agree.

- Rather than criticizing others, you are aware that you too are flawed. You will accept others just as you hope they will accept you.

- Though you try to be socially appropriate, you are not consumed with the opinions others have of you.

- You may enjoy a good competition, but winning is not everything.

If pride is the beginning of all emotional ills, humility is the beginning of emotional healthiness. True joy or contentment or patience or kindness occurs when we modestly consider our own preferences and recognize the value of following God's lead. Even confrontations can be made in humility as we do so with a desire to introduce structure to relationships that are ultimately beneficial for all.

TRUST IN GOD EAch DAy & EAch SiTuaTioN

In chapter 2 we saw that sinful pride carries the inevitable consequence of fear. As a result we are naturally defensive and are inclined to be measured in our communications and self-revelations. But we need not succumb completely to fears. While it is realistic to assume that *some* defensiveness will remain in our character, it does not have to be paramount. To set aside fear, we can learn to trust God.

Our fall into sin has left us with unwanted fears. We are uncertain of the plans and motives of other people.

The familiar passage of Proverbs 3:5–6 tells us, "Trust in the Lord with all your heart, and do not lean on your own understanding. In all your ways acknowledge Him, and He will make your paths straight." Trusting God is believing that He is the all-knowing, all-powerful sovereign Being the Bible says He is. It involves a willing submission to His teachings and directions, even if we do not fully comprehend them. Trust goes beyond mere believing. It involves doing as well as believing.

In 1980 I fractured my right femur (the large thigh bone) in two places. The pain was intense, unlike any physical pain I had ever known. I was in a desperate and needy position. And I was also very fearful. I had never had so much as a cavity, much less broken bones. Knowing that I lacked the capacity to mend my broken leg, I submitted readily to my doctor's orders. When he explained how he would have to surgically place a stainless steel rod into the femur, my response was, "Fine, when do we start?" When he told me that my poor lung condition required that I should be administered a spinal block instead of general anesthesia, I said, "You're the doctor; do whatever you must do." When he explained that I must submit to physical therapy afterward, I replied, "If that's what will help, sign me up."

I was scared to death as I contemplated the nature of this surgery, yet there I was agreeing to everything he asked me to do. Why was I so eager to trust the doctor's instructions? What other choice did I have? I was in a pitiable position. My only other choice was to remain in fear and pain, which I was unwilling to do.

In the same way, our fall into sin has left us with unwanted fears. We are uncertain of the plans and motives of other people. We face the possibility of being rejected or misunderstood or ignored or dominated. These things bother us, and rightly so. As we read Scripture, we sense God saying, "Trust Me, I'll guide you." And our reaction is skepticism. But He persists: "Follow My plans, and you'll be safe." Yet we remain unsure. Still He continues: "Look to Me; I know your needs." And we can finally conclude, "OK. What other real options do I have?"

TURNING FEAR INTO TRUST IN GOD

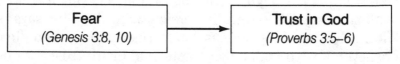

Figure 3-2

Setting aside our fears in favor of trusting God means that we will be less consumed with the worries caused by our uncertainties with others, and more consumed with living openly in the ways of decency prescribed by God. For example, suppose a middle-aged woman is extremely defensive because of the controlling spirit of her husband. He is very opinionated and prone to rejecting her if she maintains ideas or feelings different from his. Her defensiveness implies fear. She thinks, *I can't be open. He'll think I'm ludicrous for having the opinions I do.* So she plays communication games of cat-and-mouse with him.

The thought then occurs to her, *I'm a decent person. I've done nothing to bring shame upon myself. I am considerate in my dealings with my husband. I'll be more open about who I am.* Common sense would indicate that it is fully appropriate for her to let her needs and feelings be tactfully known. She need apologize for nothing. She is a legitimate person. So she decides to let go of her fearful defense in favor of authenticity. It is at this point that she can invoke her trust in God. She concludes: *If my husband chooses to think poorly of me, that is truly sad. Yet if I am to be the person God says I can be, I cannot afford to filter my every thought and feeling through his mood.* She is not abrasive, just quietly confident.

Trusting in God produces openness. When we understand that He gifts us with competence and reason, we realize that cowering in the presence of mere humans is senseless. Though we can still maintain tact in our relational styles (trusting God is not a license for arrogance), we are less consumed with the negatives given by others.

The element that makes this trust possible is faith. Faith is belief and reliance not contingent upon tangible proof. It involves the belief that we are not alone and that human frailty is not as negative as God's power is positive.

My profession pays attention to professional journals. These journals present experiments that give insights into the things that motivate people. They also contain articles attempting to prove theories about such subjects as proper child discipline, handling stress, motivating employees, and treating substance abuse. We are trained to examine such data, looking for proofs that tell us which ideas are valid or invalid.

But the Bible makes no attempt to prove that God is who He says He is or that His ways are statistically more reliable than mankind's ways. It simply assumes that God knows best —period. The believer who chooses to trust in God may never produce laboratory-perfect experiments to validate His truth. We are instead given the option to accept or reject His truth as real. Let life bear the proof.

Those who have reared preschool children can appreciate this principle. Children may not understand our intentions when we tell them to stay out of the street or go to bed at a certain time. They do not have the same capacity to comprehend the world as we do. Parents who love their children say, "Trust me." We know it is futile to conduct experiments or engage in idle debates to prove a point. Instead, we let our children know of the love behind the commandment, and we use that love as the basis to ask for trust.

In the same way, God recognizes that humans cannot possibly comprehend all His ways. So He shows us His love in the person of Jesus Christ and says, "There is no need to live in fear of your circumstances; trust Me." First John 4:18 summarizes this principle: "There is no fear in love; but perfect love casts out fear."

As we determine to fear human rejections less, trusting instead in God's guidance, we see differences in our manner of interacting with others:

- You are not worried about revealing imperfections. Authenticity is a highly cherished characteristic.
- When someone confronts you, you are willing to hear it out fully. Rebuttals are minimal.
- While you enjoy predictability, you are not so rigid that you cannot explore or allow for differences.
- Rejection by others is tempered by the fact that your acceptance by God is permanent.

• You are open to questions about your decisions. You do not mind being flexible.

As we learn to place trust in the guidance of God, we do not cease having doubts or indecision in our interactions with others. But it does mean that defensiveness and insecurity are modified by the belief that no circumstance is too threatening for God.

FELLOWSHIP

In the previous chapter we concluded that loneliness was the third major emotional struggle to result from mankind's fall into sin. A feeling of separation overcame humanity in our relationship with God, as well as with fellow humans. No one is immune from the feelings of isolation or disconnectedness.

As we grow into adulthood, we each look for ways to relieve our loneliness, whether we are consciously aware of it or not. We initiate activities with others to alleviate boredom. We attend social functions just to be near others. We even watch TV with the motivation to just stay in touch with the outside world. Many of our efforts are successful in that they make us feel wanted and connected. But many of our efforts may actually increase the struggle because they may involve immorality or contact with ultimately undesirable people.

No measure of performance can make a person successful until he learns to establish deep and satisfying relationships—first with God, then with others.

Scripture instructs how to break the grip of loneliness: by accepting God's invitation to fellowship with Him and by sharing in fellowship with like-minded believers. "Indeed our fellowship is with the Father, and with His Son Jesus Christ. . . . If we walk in the light as He Himself is in the light, we have fellowship with one another" (1 John 1:3, 7).

Fellowship is defined as a companionable relationship. It includes sharing deep personal experiences, giving and receiving love, experiencing joy with others, being united in times of need. When we fellowship with others, we are willing to relate in a wide variety of experiences and circumstances.

I often ask people to describe their ideas of success. Most people respond that success means performing the best we can in whatever we do. This reflects a performance mind-set. More theologically-minded people might say something about bringing glory to God. That is closer to the highest answer, but they still tend to have a performance orientation.

Although I do not negate those ideas, I define *success* in terms of relationships. No measure of performance can make a person successful until he learns to establish deep and satisfying relationships—first with God, then with others. Only when we are clothed in loving interchanges can we think about being successful. Although a certain amount of loneliness is inescapable, we can alleviate much of it by our willingness to engage with others.

For example, Hebrews 10:24–25 teaches us to gather together assemblies for the purpose of encouraging one another. Ecclesiastes 4:9 instructs us to join together with others so that we can give aid in times of need. Philippians 2:3–5 instructs us to follow Christ's example of looking out for the needs of others. God desires us to connect with others as a means of fending off loneliness.

Many people dig themselves into deep holes of isolation because of an unwillingness to put out the effort to join with others. This might be called relational laziness. The lonely single adult may know that he should reach out to peers but concludes, "I'd rather not make the effort." A disgruntled wife may see the need for drawing closer to her husband but says, "That hasn't gotten me anywhere before, so why try?" Such people contribute to their own loneliness.

Lessening the impact of loneliness requires a twofold mind-set. First, we must not be threatened by the reality of loneliness, since it is part of our imperfection. We should never be surprised by its presence. Second, we must set aside pride and fear, then reach out to others in fellowship.

Turning Loneliness into Fellowship

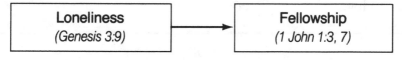

Figure 3-3

I got to know twenty-year-old divorcée Louise, who was shy and retiring. When she married out of high school, she was unprepared for marriage, as was her young husband. They quickly experienced heated arguments. On several occasions he hit her. At other times he would not come home until the middle of the night. Before their first wedding anniversary they were separated. Divorce papers were finalized a few months later. Louise went to her parents' house to hibernate, and there she spent several months seeing no one outside her immediately family.

When Louise came to my office, I could tell she was eager for something positive to happen. Though very self-conscious about her embarrassing status as a divorcée and fearful of potential judgments, she made plans to attend a nearby college. She decided to get her own apartment in order to reestablish her adult identity. Because her new circumstances had the potential for loneliness, we made plans to confront other issues. First, we examined her attitudes about herself. We realized that she could not expect instant success in finding relationships, but she determined she would not be threatened by the potential for disappointment. She made the commitment to renew her trust in God and to fellowship with Him in prayer and Bible study.

As Louise became acclimated to her new routine, she sought out the fellowship of other students. She joined a Christian group that met twice a week for meals and Bible instruction. She found a church that felt comfortable to her. She felt like the "odd man out" for a while, since no one else in her group had been through the same harrowing experiences as she. But she determined (against her natural grain) to be open, seeking to share true acceptance with people familiar with God's love.

At the core of our being,
we are each equally prone to sin
and equally loved by God.

Many times Louise felt like retreating into her old ways of seclusion and withdrawal. But, as she reminded herself of the repercussions of such a choice, she determined it was worth the effort to pursue fellowship. Even though extroversion did not come naturally to her, she persisted because she knew that Christian fellowship was the only way out of the pit of loneliness.

I admire people like Louise because they refuse to be held back by the strains produced by sin. There are countless other heroes like her, who have shed the isolation imposed by problems such as past sexual abuse or business failure or family disagreements to become successfully linked with people willing to accept and encourage. The process of breaking the hold of loneliness is not accomplished overnight, as Louise learned. But with persistence it can be minimized greatly.

Once you commit to a mind-set of fellowship, adjustments can be made in your lifestyle:

✔ When someone cannot understand you, rather than dwelling on the problem you can move on to an area of compatibility.

↙ When love needs are lacking, you can avoid illicit sexual temptation and seek out activities that will encourage wholesome relating.

↙ Though you may not be a perfect socialite, you can draw out others in conversations. You will share an interest in people regularly.

↙ You will acknowledge that grief and sadness are a way of life. These matters will be allowed emotional release, yet they will not completely debilitate you.

↙ Prayer and study of God's word will be a regular part of your life, as will fellowship with like-minded believers.

Choosing to set aside excuses that would keep you in isolation, you can decrease loneliness by maintaining constructive ties with others, as prescribed by God.

GOD-GIVEN VALUE

The fourth major emotional struggle to befall sinful mankind was inferiority. Each of us has contended in some manner with feelings of inadequacy and loneliness. Left unresolved it perpetuates battles of one-upmanship and manipulation in our closest relationships.

Realistically, we each *are* inferior. We are inferior when compared to God's perfect standard. But we are not inferior to one another. We differ in skills and achievements, with some persons making a significantly more positive impact on the world than others. Yet at the core of our being, we are each equally prone to sin and equally loved by God. Spiritually, we cannot afford to think in terms of our inferiority or superiority to one another.

Though sin plunges us into a state of inferiority, God in His mercy chooses to lift us out of such lowliness. Ever consistent, God intended that Adam would be the crowning achievement in creation, and, though Adam failed Him, God chose to continue offering the gift of worth to Adam's descendants.

Genesis 1:27 states that He created us in His image, indicating that mankind was given the ultimate high status. Psalm 8:4–5 reiterates this theme as it declares anew the value God places on His people: "What is man that you are mindful of him, the son of man that you care for him? You made him a little lower than the heavenly beings and crowned him with glory and honor" (NIV).

The psalmist struggled with his identity just as we do today. Surely he compared himself with others and repeatedly felt that he came up short. He might notice how others were more consistent in positive qualities such as patience or kindness. Perhaps he flinched when he noticed how others handled family matters more smoothly than he did. Or it could have been that he anguished as he considered the many secret sins in his thoughts that were too embarrassing to be publicly known. He was just like you and me.

In his quiet moments of reflection he wondered, *Why would God concern Himself with someone like me? Who am I to be the recipient of any mercy from Him? I've got so many hang-ups, it's humiliating!* But the Lord revealed to him then, just as He will to us today, "You can do nothing to stop me from loving you; that's not my style. In the beginning I created humanity to bear My image, and I continue to do so. You are Mine, and I will privilege you with the ability to share in My forever kingdom."

TURNING INFERIORITY INTO GOD-GIVEN VALUE

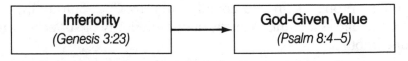

Figure 3-4

The honor of bearing the glory of God is not the reward for good behavior, nor is it something that comes and goes on the basis of our performances. This gift of majestic value is offered to us, unmerited, by the God of love, who chooses to reveal part of His character to us in this unique manner. Our sinful inclination causes us to struggle with feelings of inadequacy, yet God has responded, "Though you have let Me down, I continue to regard you as highly worthy." We are lifted from our inferiority feelings as we accept this proclamation as true.

This concept of God-given value is so elementary it seems too good to be true. Consequently, many feel that they should do something—anything—to prove their value. They assume that they must be emotionally stable or morally pure or spiritually mature before God will *really* esteem them. They humanize God and, consequently, detract from His divine nature by assuming that His ways are mankind's ways.

Scott, the man mentioned at the beginning of this chapter, had struggled with his feelings of adequacy largely because he was extremely focused on how his achievements caused him to compare with others. In his childhood he had learned to be a people-pleaser, keeping an eye out for the approval of both peers and authorities. He had excelled in sports, with his father serving as a strong driving force. In his adult years he felt he could earn personal value by making lots of money, having an impressive title, and accomplishing impressive deeds in his church and community. Yet, in spite of his efforts, Scott was perpetually unsure of himself. His mistake was in seeking his value in the wrong places.

I asked Scott to tell me what he assumed God thought about him. Predictably, he admitted that he did not like to think much about God since he pictured Him as a harsh, foreboding figure. When I told him that God was holy beyond our comprehension yet compassionate toward sinners, he responded, "I wish I could believe that."

Scott was familiar with the Bible, so I asked him to take a week to read the gospel of John. If he read three chapters a day, he could complete the twenty-one chapters of the book in that amount of time. I wanted him to focus on the depth of love Christ portrayed to those who knew Him.

Later, when he and I met, he remarked how astonished he was at the encouragement Jesus offered common people. "Do you really believe that's the way God is?" he asked. I assured him that Christ's mission was to embody the love of God the Father so that His character would no longer be as mysterious.

Shortly afterward, Scott made the decision to let Jesus become his Savior, accepting the value and worth that came with it. At that point, he and I discussed how his lifestyle could be altered so that he would no longer be obsessed with his standing with others but live in a way that declared his feelings of adequacy. When people like Scott choose to live in the truth of their God-given value, their behavior and responses change:

- They are willing to apologize when necessary, yet they will not be chronically apologetic.
- Knowing that their worth is a gift from God, they will not feel compelled to perform for it.
- While they will desire personal excellence, they will not be shocked to discover their inadequacies.
- Knowing of their forgiveness by God, they'll not be unduly concerned with others' inability to forgive.
- Conversations are not a competition to "one-up" another person. They can assume equality at all times.

KINDHEARTEDNESS

The fifth major emotional problem resulting from the fall into sin is anger. Can't you imagine the bickering between Adam and Eve as they tried to make sense of their rapid loss of status? As they turned into accusers toward one another, the need for self-preservation was born. Though it is natural, and sometimes good, to stand firmly for personal needs in the face of rejection, the anger we experience easily becomes aggressive.

There has been a great push in the world of psychology to stand assertively for oneself in the face of unwarranted strains. Indeed, the Bible backs this thought to a certain extent. Ephesians 4:26 tells us, "Be angry, and yet do not sin." James 1:19 cautions to be "slow to anger," with the implication that anger may sometimes serve a proper function as long as we are judicious in our use of it.

Whereas aggressive anger is the by-product of a mind absorbed in pride, kindheartedness is the result of a mind committed to humility.

Nonetheless, sinfulness easily causes us to cross the line of true assertive anger into the realm of harmful anger. It is easy to feel so agitated that we are in need of an internal governor that keeps our anger from degenerating to an ugly extreme. That internal governor is kindness.

Ephesians 4:31 points out several forms of anger that we are to set aside: bitterness, wrath, clamor, slander, and malice. Then verse 32 instructs, "Be kind one to another, tender-hearted, forgiving each other, just as God in Christ also has forgiven you."

Whereas aggressive anger is the by-product of a mind absorbed in pride, kindheartedness is the result of a mind committed to humility. To be kindhearted means that there is a natural desire to give pleasure and to do good. It is characterized by a mild, gentle nature that desires joy in encouraging others. Kindheartedness may not be something we are naturally inclined toward, yet it can be a regular feature of a life guided by the Holy Spirit.

To arrive at kindheartedness, we must have a successful game plan for dealing with anger. We can be aware of the unhealthy options regarding anger: repressing it, being openly aggressive with it, being passively aggressive. Yet we can conclude that these options are genuinely undesirable. Instead, we can be committed to doing whatever it takes to keep a clean emotional slate. This involves two general ways of managing anger: being appropriately assertive, and knowing when to let go of it in favor of forgiveness or acceptance.

For instance, suppose you had a history of rejection from your own father. Perhaps he was hypercritical or insensitive. You have harbored anger, understandably so, for the lack of regard he communicated. Through the years you cling to this emotion, wishing he could have been a real daddy. At some point, there needs to be an end to the anger. It may come as you talk with him about your feelings of the past. Or perhaps you can learn to communicate for the first time as a coequal with him. It could be that you will discover that he will never change, which will then prompt you to regrettably accept him for what he is. This implies a willingness to forgive.

Turning Anger into Kindheartedness

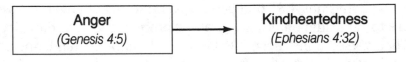

Figure 3-5

At any rate, there is a time when your anger needs to give way to something new, something beneficial to yourself and to those you love. This is where kindheartedness enters. While you may have an excuse to feel angry, you conclude, "I'd rather not be a prisoner to painful emotions. It's time to move on."

By stating that kindheartedness is preferred over anger, I imply that I have a choice regarding my emotional status. The person who recognizes that anger has outlived its usefulness can set it aside in favor of a more appropriate trait. That does not mean that the anger is repressed in order to feign pleasantness. Rather, there is a deliberate disconnection from that which has created the inner turmoil. Also, kindheartedness is not the result of a one-time decision. Anger, regarding past or recurring circumstances, has a way of returning to the personality repeatedly. Therefore, today I can make a deliberate decision to be guided by kindheartedness, knowing that tomorrow I may be required to reevaluate my emotions and make the same decision again.

As I write these words, I am reminded that my own family history is full of struggles with anger. My father's father was harsh and negative. He directed criticism and rejection toward anyone who did not measure up to his strict standards. My own father was keenly aware of how easily we each could slip into anger, so he repeatedly instructed me about the excesses of anger. Part of his "therapy" included discussing with his offspring the need to appeal to God for kindness and grace. I was impressed with such leadership. By recognizing his options, he had chosen to take a different route than his own father. I have chosen to do the same.

When you make the decision to set aside anger in favor of kindheartedness, new behaviors and attitudes emerge:

- You will yield as often as possible to the positive, which comes from the Lord.
- Though minor problems are indeed annoying, you do not dwell on them long.
- Forgiveness is not contingent on others' behavior. It is a choice.
- Rather than envying others, you can focus on what is good in your life, dwelling in contentment.
- You can allow for down moods, while choosing not to be dominated by them.
- Openness, rather than withdrawal, will be a natural part of your conflict resolution.

THE PROGRESSION OF RESOLUTIONS

Since the five major emotional struggles can be understood to feed into each other with a domino effect, we can assume that the resolutions to those problems are also progressive. Figure 3-6 illustrates this.

Kindheartedness, at the bottom of the chart, cannot be attained on its own. It requires that we first comprehend our God-given value. But this cannot occur if we are not in fellowship with God and other believers. However, that fellowship implies that we have chosen first to trust God. But that trust is contingent on the decision to set self aside in humility.

As you seek to implement the truths given in Scripture, acknowledge that you will not achieve perfection. That will not occur until you pass through heaven's gates. Rather, your growth will be ongoing.

In the next five chapters, we will explore how our efforts to resolve the emotions of sinfulness can be thwarted by environmental pressures. We may have success in learning the biblical answers to our emotional problems, yet we will also need to learn how to reconcile the problems caused by the imperfections the world perpetuates. By working through those psychological barriers, we will understand how ultimate healing is the result of successfully addressing our spiritual and psychological problems.

THE PROGRESSION OF RESOLUTIONS

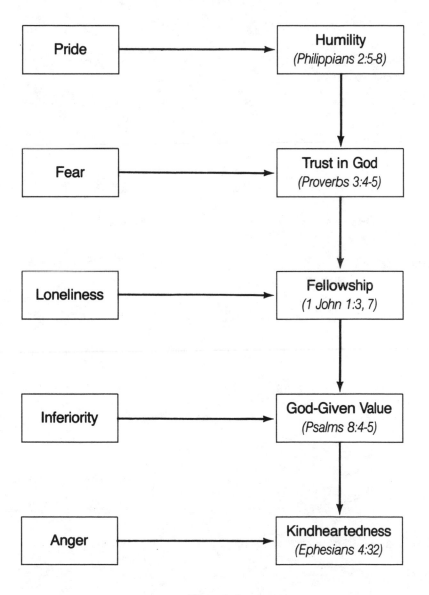

Figure 3-6

Part 2

Psychological Barriers
to Personal Growth

4

THE BARRIER OF DEFICIENT LOVE

I already know what the Bible says I'm supposed to do, so why do I still have so many problems?" I have heard Christians ask that question countless times. It's a good question, and it deserves a good answer.

In the last two chapters we examined how our emotional strains originated with the fall into sin. Were it not for mankind's inherent tendency to defy God, we would have none of the tensions that threaten to undermine the foundations of our personal well-being. So before we can find peace we each must privately come to terms with our sins and seek God's direction for a new way of life.

As mentioned in chapter 1, I do not want to be guilty of offering simplistic, legalistic-sounding solutions to our emotional problems. It is not enough to say that if we get our thoughts lined up with Scripture our lives will fall into perfect order. Don't misunderstand. I genuinely believe that a life in Christ is the only life truly pleasing to God. But I am aware that many Christians have problems that do not go away with increased Bible study and prayer. This is where insight into some of the psychological factors comes into play.

THE NEED FOR LOVE

Matthew 22:35–39 records the familiar conversation between a young lawyer and Jesus. The Lord is asked to identify the greatest of the commandments. You know His response. The chief aim of life is to love. We are to love God with all our hearts, souls, and minds, and to love others as ourselves. Life becomes satisfying when we know love, and it is incomplete when love is deficient. Because love is the most basic of all needs, we experience emotional pain in its absence just as surely as we feel hunger without food. Emotional turmoil can be interpreted as a cry for love.

The first of our psychological barriers to personal growth, then, is deficient love experiences. It keeps us stuck in the emotions produced by sin.

THE BARRIER OF DEFICIENT LOVE EXPERIENCES

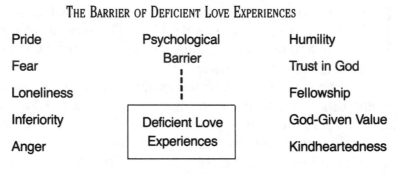

Pride	Psychological	Humility
Fear	Barrier	Trust in God
Loneliness		Fellowship
Inferiority	Deficient Love	God-Given Value
Anger	Experiences	Kindheartedness

Figure 4-1

Developmental psychologists agree on the universal need for love. Infants communicate only at the simplest level, yet they can let us know when they feel or do not feel loved. Studies have shown that depriving an infant of consistent love is devastating to his emotional, intellectual, and physical development. Without successful experiences of giving and receiving love early in life, it is difficult for us to establish trust and closeness in later relationships. Some studies have even suggested that a child can die in the more extreme incidences of lost love.

Consider each of the primary relationships, and you will easily discover how love is a crucial element in aiding a person who is lacking emotional stability. For instance, the love of a father toward his children is central to a young person's ability to discover godly composure. In the great high priestly prayer recorded in John 17, Jesus spoke to God, saying, "I manifested Thy name to the men whom Thou gavest Me" (v. 6). Such a statement might catch a casual reader off guard. "I thought everyone knew God's name," might be the response.

In the Old Testament, God was known by many descriptive titles, but it was not until Jesus' ministry that God's personal name was fully revealed: *Father.* Jesus taught that God could be known as a father figure to those believing in Him. He would be the ultimate authority figure, yet as approachable as one's daddy. He would be tuned in to His offspring. He would take time out to handle the trivial aggravations. He would be an open, familiar figure. Knowing the fatherly love of God would be a key component in finding inner peace and stability. He would be our place of security.

Now that Jesus has revealed the name of God as *Father,* the job of showing that manner of godly, secure love is entrusted to real dads. It is there that problems may occur. Some fathers have taken seriously their task of giving their young the feeling of acceptance. They establish a nurturing leadership and encourage confidences and stability in their children.

But other fathers have not fared as well. Some are openly hostile toward their children, giving abuse or being chronically condescending. Others may take lightly their role and simply ignore their children's emotional needs, leaving that task solely to the mother. Others may be well intended—they are active in the child's life, but they are clueless as to how to respond well to tender emotions or anxious moments.

When fatherly love is deficient, the child may hear concepts about living in humility or finding God-given worth, but it does not seem real. Before the idea can germinate and grow in the young mind, it needs to be experienced. The lack of that experience keeps the young child imprisoned in the emotions of the sin nature.

A mother's love for a child is of equal importance to that of the father. An Old Testament description of God's character is *El Shaddai.* Some language scholars tell us that the term *shad* could be rendered "breast." *El Shaddai* means "God Our Strength," in the sense that a mother exhibits a powerful strength as she nurses her young. As long as that mother is near, the child can feel completely protected.

The mother's designated role is to provide a comforting strength to her developing children. She is to be available as a "home base" for the child as he or she gradually learns to interact with the surrounding world. She can be most instrumental in instilling confidence in the child by teaching proficiencies in the many social skills required to get along successfully with others. She can be sensitive to emotions, teaching her young the fine balance between accepting themselves for what they are, even as they learn to be proficient in managing errant feelings. As the mother succeeds in these functions, the child can more readily grow in the qualities that represent maturity.

---

*These three relationships
—father, mother, and spouse—
are the most common places for
deficient love to be experienced.*

As I counsel with adults in the midst of emotional pain, many can look backward and sadly conclude that Mother did not fully exhibit the qualities that would create the atmosphere of comforting strength. This is due to any number of reasons. Perhaps she suffered from her own emotional turmoil, which inhibited her from responding to her children's needs. Maybe her marriage was in disrepair and she felt burdened with playing both mother and father roles. Perhaps she was sidetracked by alcoholism or other drugs, or maybe she simply felt confused regarding the traits of a successful parent.

When a mother is deficient in offering godly love, the child is not necessarily doomed to emotional trauma, but he may find emotional peace elusive. The child already has his own sin nature to contend with. He may also have his mother's inconsistencies to sift through as a part of the effort to feel whole.

A third major relationship intended to illustrate godly love is the marriage. Ephesians 5:22–33 describes a healthy marriage as being parallel to Christ's love for His own. First Peter 3:1–7 gives further encouragement to spouses, and the passage ends with the phrase "so that your prayers may not be hindered." The implication is that when husbands and wives are synchronized they have a more natural capacity to live in the stability of God's love. Revelation 21:1–4 describes the futuristic scene of Christ returning for His church as a groom would receive his bride. Again, the implication is that a husband-wife relationship could ideally illustrate Christ's manner of love.

When spouses are in harmony in their love relationship, they can show one another worth and respect in a way no other relationship can. As they see each other in the broad array of strengths and weaknesses, honoring each other even in the midst of imperfection, they become grace bearers. The love is powerful enough to bring out the very best in each other. Stability is experienced. Peace and patience and kindness are relatively natural.

But what can be said when the marriage relationship is sour—or perhaps when a divorce occurs? Or what of the single person who desires marriage but is rebuffed in that realm? Since marriage is such a key element in helping a person find emotional balance, it stands to reason that a deficient love experience in this regard can increase the potential for emotional duress. Questions of doubt enter the mind. Rejection feelings are registered. Anger is felt. The individual can feel stuck in an unwanted trap of emotional despair.

These three relationships—father, mother, and spouse—are the most common places for deficient love to be experienced. But deficient love can result from other painful relationships as well. The role of brother and sister ideally should demonstrate caring and regard, which would enable persons to more easily find personal peace. But when strains are experienced among siblings, it detracts from an individual's overall well-being. The same could be said for relationships among friends as well as for interactions with church leaders.

DEPENDENCY BECOMES IMBALANCED

We can assert that because we each have a need to be loved in all of our major relationships, dependency is an integral part of the human personality. God has created us to have internal reactors that detect our standing with others, and, when that standing is solid, we feel secure. When that standing is weak or missing, we feel less stable. Dependency is defined as the tendency for inner emotions to be swayed by external circumstances.

Not only is dependency not a bad trait, it is very normal. There is no person who experiences zero dependency. It can be understood as the glue that holds relationships together.

Dependency imbalances result, though, when one or more significant relationships falter. For example, the girl whose father or mother was harsh or rejecting can become a woman who is too consumed with the opinions of others. Rather than drawing upon an inner sense of emotional composure, she may feel anxious or easily annoyed or fearful. Her deficient love experiences have caused her to question her personal legitimacy. Instead of feeling secure in the knowledge that people consider her valuable, her emotions become insecure. "If my father was not consistently loving," she might reason, "I wonder who else will reject me."

Notice in the following examples how deficient love can cause emotional stability to depend too heavily on people and circumstances:

- A husband with a history of tension with his father is easily angered when his wife and children question his decisions. He has difficulty expressing warmth.

- A teenager feels chronically misunderstood by his parents, so he turns to "the crowd" for approval.

- A wife and mother feels unappreciated by her family and sinks into a deep depression.

- A husband feels dissatisfied in his love relationship with his wife and turns to a mistress for affection.

- A woman was sexually abused by a stepfather and is guarded in her interactions with others, especially men.

- A businessman senses disapproval from co-workers and puts extra pressure on his family to make him feel secure.

Each of these illustrations involved deficient love experiences from significant others. The result is imbalanced dependency. Lacking fulfillment, their emotions carry them to out-of-bounds habits.

THE EFFECT ON THE BASIC EMOTIONS

We have established that each person has a natural predisposition toward emotional upheaval because of the Fall. But notice how those emotions can become even more prominent with deficient love experiences.

Pride: As persons sense that proper love is not forthcoming, they become increasingly self-preoccupied. "Hey, what about me?" becomes a standard cry. Feeling desperate and out of control, they may resort to various means to force love. For example, a rejected spouse may angrily demand respect. Or an adult with a history of missed love may become manipulative in the effort to make others respond to her as she would like. Consciously or subconsciously the thought emerges: *If others will not love me as I want, I'll do whatever I must to feel satisfied.*

Fear: Rejections from significant others increase the tendency to be defensive. Humans already have an inherent tendency to be guarded in the fear that others may be rejecting or untrustworthy. But a major disappointment in a key relationship can cause fear to be all the more prominent. Self-doubt becomes more prevalent as the thought is nurtured, *I wonder who else might not love me.* Deficient love creates a sinking feeling that they cannot afford to be open with others. Rather than feeling confident, they approach others with hidden insecurities.

Ultimately the experience of deficient love feeds the tendency toward anger.

Loneliness: God created humans to be connected, but deficient love experiences create the feeling of disconnectedness. Sin has already given each person a taste of isolation, but rejection only causes the gulf between individuals to widen. The increased sense of loneliness can be manifested in increased feelings of sadness or in deeper yearnings for sexual intimacy or in unusual difficulty accepting the loss of those who have proven reliable. When persons experience deficient love, they anguish more deeply with the question of how to be rid of the sensation of alienation.

Inferiority: Ideally, rewarding love experiences enhance individuals' ability to find inner worth and strength. But when that love is missing, the inborn struggle with inferiority becomes even more powerful. People who have felt rejected more naturally nurse guilt: "Is there something I should have done to get others to love me?" They can become self-critical in comparing themselves with others, thinking that they must possess hidden flaws that others do not. To compensate for these feelings of rejection, many will attempt to find ways of establishing superiority. They may develop perfectionism, workaholism, achievement obsessions, or domineering ways.

Anger: Ultimately the experience of deficient love feeds the tendency toward anger. Angry individuals are questioning why others refuse to accept them as worthy or respectable. The anger is a protest that enables these people to advocate their personal needs that are ignored by others. But when love is deficient, the anger usually extends beyond the boundaries of healthiness. A demanding pattern can emerge, as can an uncooperative spirit. Bitterness and depression can settle in as these persons become increasingly pessimistic about the prospects of receiving desirable love interchanges. The anger in them backfires as it insures that the love they are demanding will never be given.

OVERCOMING DEFICIENT LOVE EXPERIENCES

Once rejection has taken its toll on a person's feelings of emotional stability, its effects may be difficult to reconcile. When people are attempting to overcome deficient love, they cannot just flip a switch and declare, "I'll just memorize the characteristics of a healthy Christian and live in those traits forevermore."

Change takes time. Reorienting the mind in the aftermath of love disappointments is not automatic. But it can be done. The messages given by humans are not final. Humans are not the ultimate source of truth or strength. To overcome the emotional strains of deficient love, we can develop spiritual well-being.

OVERCOMING DEFICIENT LOVE EXPERIENCES

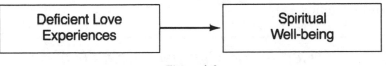

Figure 4-2

On the day of your birth, value was present. Immediately someone cared for you. You were wrapped in a blanket and held. You were given attention from many sources. As the days passed, you were fed, clothed, and sheltered. No one was forced to be loving to you. People loved you merely because you existed. You had made no A's on a report card nor had you starred on any athletic team. You were incapable of proving your value, yet responsible adults instinctively recognized that you had inherent worth.

When Scripture teaches that we are each created in God's image, it implies that we have a special designation given by God. It has nothing to do with performances, nor is it dependent upon humans recognizing it. You have worth because God declares you to be worthy.

Now think carefully. When humans choose not to acknowledge the worth bestowed on you by God, does that mean it ceases to exist? Not at all. Though God gave fathers, mothers, spouses, siblings, and friends the responsibility to demonstrate His love, that love is not rendered void when humans fail. When humans offer deficient love experiences, it does not mean that you no longer are worthy before God; it only illustrates that humans are fallible.

When the negative emotions dominate a personality, as they inevitably do in the wake of deficient love experiences, concrete facts have a way of being lost in the shuffle. For instance, the woman feeling shameful because her father was abusive is so wrapped up in her feelings that she forgets (if in fact she even knew at all) that she has inherent worth. When this is the case, there must be a willingness to set aside the emotions long enough to become grounded in the facts. The Bible refers to this as transformation by the renewing of the mind (Romans 12:2).

Deep inside your personality is a "worth mechanism" that instinctively responds to the way people treat you.

How can a person who has felt unloved know that there is a guaranteed value given him or her by God? Consider an undeniable instinct in each of us. You have a wide range of emotions, both positively and negatively charged. The negative emotions appear in the face of maltreatment or rejection or neglect. If you were an inherently worthless person, and you knew it through and through, would you ever feel anger or tension in the presence of mistreatment? No, you would feel nothing. Your emotions would be flat because you would be thinking, *So what if people abuse me; they're only telling me what I already know.*

Or turn the illustration around. If you were a completely worthless person, and you knew it, would you ever experience joy or peace when people were kind to you? Again the answer is no. If you were worthless you would think, *I don't see why anyone would want to be pleasant to me; I have nothing to offer.*

But in fact, you do feel frustrated when treated poorly. You do enjoy it when others reinforce you. Why? Because you have inherent value! Deep inside your personality is a "worth mechanism" that instinctively responds to the way people treat you. That worth mechanism knows when it is being over-looked —thus the negative emotions. It also knows when it has been satisfactorily touched—thus the positive emotions. This worth mechanism has been in you from the day of birth. It is not learned; it is God-given.

The apostle Paul understood that it was necessary to live in a knowledge of inherent worth as the foundation for his emotional stability. Philippians 4:11 records his well-known words: "I have learned to be content in whatever circumstances I am." He had determined that he could not afford to lean on the unpredictable nature of family and friends. They were too fickle. So, instead, he drew his strength from a spiritual base. He knew he had value before God, and that is what mattered most.

Keep in mind that Paul did not have an easy life, nor was his history exclusively positive. Paul had many rejections weighing him down. We could easily surmise that his childhood was quite strict. He was born into an aristocratic home, where rules were far more important than feelings. He had been tutored by Gamaliel in what was regarded as the Harvard of his day. He had been the rising star as a young Pharisee, known for his brilliant mind, if not also for his ruthless manner of dealing with opponents.

Paul had also been an angry young man, so much so that he would seek out Christians to have them murdered. This contempt must have been fueled by an incredible insecurity, though undoubtedly he never would have admitted it at the time. He was a controlling, hate-filled man bent on doing whatever it took to climb the ladder.

Imagine the shake-up in his world when he dramatically converted to Christianity. Though our information regarding the establishment's reaction to him is sketchy, we can easily determine that he was excommunicated. The man who had been a rising star was now a pitiable, hated reject. He was a Benedict Arnold. There is a good likelihood that all ties were severed with his family. Though he refers to many friends in his epistles, he never mentions family. He had been a Pharisee, who traditionally had to be married. But we know he was a single man during his ministry. Could it be that his wife and children abandoned him, branding him as a lunatic or heretic?

Even his acceptance among Christians was shaky. While Paul had some fiercely loyal companions, he also had powerful enemies, in and out of the church. Through the years he had been whipped with lashes five times, beaten with rods three times, stoned and left for dead. Riots began in many cities because of controversies surrounding his teachings. He often went without adequate food and clothing.

But then, in a prison cell, we see Paul penning the words, "I have learned to be content in whatever circumstances I am." How could he say this? He had determined that his worth was not dependent upon human initiative. Each person rejecting him had an agenda keeping them from being truly objective regarding his inner value. Therefore, his well-being became a spiritual matter to him. He would accept the evidences of God's love for him over any human input. Realizing how inaccurate and fickle people could be in their treatment of him, he acknowledged God's judgment as the sole source of truth.

I have spoken with many people who have heard the concept of spiritual well-being, but it is not real to them. They are so caught in the ongoing anguish of feeling unloved by a human that the news of God's love seems too much like a "fairy tale." Their task, which is not simple, will be to acknowledge that fallible humans cannot be given such a God-like power that they can dictate a fictional perspective on life. The recipient of deficient love needs to tell himself that human rejection does not represent ultimate truth. Compared to God's declarations, it need not stand as the ultimate basis for personal peace.

When you develop a foundation of spiritual well-being as an antidote to deficient love, your responses to rejection will be different. You will be less dependent. Notice how the following responses differ from the illustrations mentioned earlier in this chapter:

• A husband with a history of rejection from his father is not obliged to be tense when his wife and children disagree with him. He determines that disagreements are inevitable, and, even if they are not handled perfectly by his family, he can choose to respond with respect.

• A teenager may feel chronically misunderstood by his parents, but, instead of turning to "the crowd" for approval, he can choose to accept his parents as the humans they are.

• A wife and mother may feel unappreciated by her family, but, rather than sinking into a depression, she can more assertively explain her needs and delegate household chores.

• A husband feels dissatisfied with his wife, but, instead of turning to a mistress, he realizes that ultimately it is his responsibility to be a leader in the home, exhibiting traits such as kindness or loyalty or calm firmness.

• A woman with a history of sexual abuse from her stepfather can realize that one man's treatment of her does not represent the sum total of her self-evaluation. She does not have to be completely guarded with every man who gets close to her.

• A businessman who senses disapproval from co-workers does not need to pressure his family for acceptance. Instead, he acknowledges that his worth remains stable whether his colleagues choose to like him or not.

Maintaining a mind of spiritual well-being is not natural, since we are each bearers of the sin nature, meaning that we are easily carnal in our thoughts. It requires a day-by-day, event-by-event yieldedness to God. Rather than telling yourself that you will never worry again about the rejections in your life, determine how you will respond to rejections *today*. Break your day down into various events and ask, "How would I tend to respond to the lack of love that might come from my spouse? My children? My companions?" Then give yourself an assignment: "Today, how will I yield my events to God in such a way that would indicate His hand in my life."

By developing an awareness of how deficiencies hinder your emotional growth, and by determining to exercise more consciously your spiritual alternatives, you will find that your moods do not have to depend on people and circumstances.

5

THE BARRIER OF TRAINED INCOMPETENCE

During my teen years I was employed in the medical profession. I washed dishes in a hospital kitchen. Those days I was loaded with money, or so it seemed. I was able to pay for my first car and provide all the expenses for my social life. I had it made.

One advantage of such wealth was that I did not have to do my own mechanical auto work. "I'm all thumbs when it comes to that type of work," I'd say. So whenever my Ford needed work, I'd take it in to Jack's Repair Shop and pay him to do what I could not.

But my college years were different. I was perennially broke. Whatever money I'd made was already spoken for before it was earned. I still had my Ford, and it still needed repairs. But no longer in the medical profession, I had to scrape for the money to hire someone to do my dirty work. That's when a buddy goaded me: "Les, you've got the capacity to do your own car repairs. And besides, it's a lot less expensive. I'll show you what you need to do, then you can take care of your needs on your own."

I learned that when I said, "I can't do this," it was really a case of "I've never learned how." Those are two entirely different thoughts.

When people come to my counseling office, they complain of all sorts of emotional breakdowns. Depression, anxiety, anger, and insecurity are issues I hear about every day. An overwhelming number of my patients begin counseling with the mind-set of "I can't handle these emotions." Internally, my response is, "Who told you that?"

Think of the many ways you use the word *can't* as it relates to emotional or relational issues:

- I can't take it if you reject me one more time.
- When your emotions become too strong, I can't respond in a good way.
- I can't communicate my feelings as well as other people.

Even the most optimistic people can get caught in the trap of defeat when they are required to make sense of their own or someone else's emotions. Bewilderment dominates the personality, creating unnecessary turmoil.

I often tell patients, "If *can't* is true, we may as well fold up our tents and go home." *Can't* is a very definitive word. It has a ring of finality. And—it is usually a lie.

THE LACK OF TRAINING IN MANAGING EMOTIONS

There is a reason people succumb to this mind-set of defeat. It is learned through our interactions with significant others. Usually it is passed along unknowingly. Yet in the end, we are trained to think incompetently regarding personal and emotional issues.

Consider the things in life for which we receive special training. The list could be endless. Children are trained to read and write, to ride bicycles, to add and multiply, draw and sing. Teenagers are trained to drive, to do household chores, to write themes, to operate computers, and to play sports. Adults are trained to learn complex business procedures, to manage finances, keep up cars, and juggle complicated schedules. Much of the routine of modern living is boiled down to knowing the how-tos of our particular tasks.

But how much training have most of us had in understanding and managing emotions? How many hours of discussion did we have with parents or teachers regarding the goals and philosophies of communication? How many times did people show love to us while explaining that such love could draw us into a deeper understanding of God's consistent love?

The answer to these questions is painfully obvious. Most people have little or no training in the things of life that matter most. They may have been told what to do, but that is a different matter.

Think back to your childhood.
Why were emotional issues
not openly discussed?

True composure and contentment can occur only as individuals comprehend God's plan for an abundant life. This comprehension can then lead to an aware application. Many people may be able to recite various facts and theories about correct living, but knowing God's plan goes far beyond mere memorization of ideas. Facts and theories cannot be considered integrated into our lives until they directly influence the thoughts that guide our emotions and behaviors. Before that happens we must understand how scriptural truth is truly pertinent to a variety of lifestyle issues.

Consider for a moment the many subjects addressed in the Bible that are meant to enhance your quality of life. Then ask yourself how much training you have received in these areas:

✔ Balancing self-esteem with proper doses of humility
✔ Choosing to set aside difficult emotions, such as worry or fear or bitterness

✔ Letting God direct positive emotions, such as peace or patience

✔ Knowing how to be principled while also accepting others who hold different values

✔ Knowing when to be assertive and when to be silent

✔ Discerning when to serve and when to let others serve you

✔ Expressing love to others in a satisfying and fulfilling way

✔ Communicating with empathy

✔ Responding to the improper communications of others without adding to the problem

✔ Developing spiritual gifts in a manner most pleasing to God

This list could go on and on. My point is that there are many elements of successful living that need to be openly addressed if we are to find personal stability. But few people have actually been trained in these matters, meaning that the word *can't* is common in the midst of emotionally charged circumstances.

Think back to your childhood. Why were emotional issues not openly discussed? Several reasons stand out. Mom and Dad may have been preoccupied at the time with very demanding projects. Perhaps they just did not know how to talk deeply about personal issues; it was probably lacking in their own families of origin. Or perhaps they felt overwhelmed by your emotions; personal matters were a threat. It could have been that they had such a need for order that performances took priority over feelings.

You can see that it takes time and skill to help a child grasp the meaning of emotions. Children are usually capable of learning about such things if someone will help them. But, instead, parents and teachers and other authority figures are more often interested in telling the child *what to do* rather than training him *how to think*.

Look carefully at the following illustrations and notice the focus in each case. An emotion is expressed, but it is met by a response intended to quickly squelch it:

- A schoolboy complains that he is angry with the amount of homework given by his teacher. His mother tells him that being angry will do him no good; he should get started on his homework earlier. She does not take time to understand his feelings or ask him what he plans to do with his anger.
- A wife expresses bewilderment with the way her two children are constantly bickering. Her husband tells her that she should send them to their rooms for an hour and threaten to ground them if they misbehave further. No effort is made to discuss the reason for her emotions or her further options regarding the situation.
- A woman expresses frustration to a friend about a problem with a co-worker. Rather than listening understandingly and expressing confidence that she will be able to handle the situation well, the friend tells her she should look for a new job and be rid of the problem forever.

Do you see the trend? Each person in the illustrations expresses an emotion, then someone immediately tells him or her how to tie it down. When we share our problems with others, we tend to receive one thing consistently in return—unsolicited advice. Our world seems obsessed with the notion that feelings must hurriedly be resolved with ready-made solutions.

Whenever unsolicited advice is given, a deeper communication is made: "I doubt that you have the ability to handle your problem correctly, so do yourself a favor and do as I say." It is an insult. Admittedly the advisor may not be sending such a message intentionally, but once spoken the damage is done.

As you feel uncomfortable in
your ability to manage emotions,
your defenses rise.

Recall incidences from your own past. Authority figures may have been willing to give answers to your problems, but without encouraging the development of your own problem-solving skills. For example, you may have had a parent who told you how to resolve sibling disputes but was unwilling to take the time to help you sift through the emotions involved. I have spoken with many adults who as children never really knew they had choices regarding their manner of settling personal issues. Or perhaps you had teachers who were more concerned with training compliance than eliciting original thought. Maybe in your adult life you have been exposed to others (a spouse, a friend, a co-worker) who felt the need to tie down your emotional loose ends when, in fact, you needed a listening ear more than anything else.

The more exposure you have to this quick resolution manner of interaction, the more it can feed a feeling of incompetence. Most of the solutions offered have a way of oversimplifying the problem at hand. But you can be left wondering why you just can't seem to make matters fit into neat packages as your answer-giver would lead you to believe is possible.

Over time this message of incompetence increases your inclination toward the emotions inherent in you because of the sin nature:

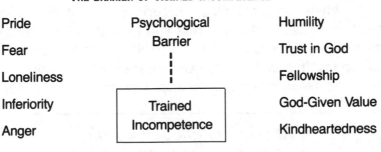

THE BARRIER OF TRAINED INCOMPETENCE

Pride	Psychological Barrier	Humility
Fear		Trust in God
Loneliness		Fellowship
Inferiority	Trained Incompetence	God-Given Value
Anger		Kindheartedness

Figure 5-1

Pride: When you are left without a game plan regarding emotional management, your thoughts eventually settle on self. You become very conscientious about errors you might make.

You feel out of control, which causes you to crave control in an unhealthy way. For example, when a family member is uncooperative, leaving you wondering what to do next, you think, *Look at how this is ruining my day. I just wish for once I could figure out how to get him to consider my needs.* Your self-focus then increases the likelihood that matters will worsen.

Fear: As you feel uncomfortable in your ability to manage emotions, your defenses rise. You do not want others to realize how inept you feel, so you cover up as best you can. This implies a lack of trust in others. Your cautious manner communicates that you feel that rejection may be an increased possibility.

Loneliness: When you lack the competence to manage emotions or relationships fully, feelings of estrangement enter your emotional disposition. When conflicts or hurts are not adequately settled, you sense a gap in the understanding between yourself and others. For instance, if a husband and wife repeatedly experience the same tensions as they futilely attempt to communicate needs, they eventually think, *What's the use* They can then settle into a routine of avoiding emotionally laden discussions.

Inferiority: A sense of competence in emotional matters can go a long way toward giving an individual a feeling of equality with others. But if you stumble in your efforts to handle such matters, you become more inclined toward feelings of inadequacy. You may rate yourself unfavorably as compared to others who seem not to have the same problems. Guilt may pile up as you ask, "What's wrong with my problem-solving skills?" To compensate you may try to portray a false superiority.

Anger: Feelings of emotional incompetence create a natural inclination toward anger. As an illustration just think of the frustration you felt the last time you struggled with a home-improvement project. When we reach the end of our resources in problem solving, we may harbor feelings of bitterness for having been placed in undesirable circumstances. We can become blaming and critical. Impatience erupts.

We already have a natural predisposition toward these five major emotions. But when our histories are lacking in the provision for internally based problem solving, they become all the more intense.

CONTEMPLATIVE THINKING

You may be thinking, *I admit it. I never had much training regarding personal issues. I've not taken the time out to determine the meaning of my emotions. But what can I do at this point in my life?*

It is preferable that emotional competence be learned in the early years, but, if that was not the case, it is still not too late. Trained incompetence can be overcome by contemplative thinking.

OVERCOMING TRAINED INCOMPETENCE

Figure 5-2

Psalm 119:97–98 records the psalmist's delight: "O how I love Thy law! It is my meditation all the day. Thy commandments make me wiser than my enemies, for they are ever mine." The writer of these words was confident in the face of tensions because he had taken the time to think through God's laws to the extent that he felt a type of ownership of them. They were more than words to him. They were well-conceived ideas.

Too many adults can look back to their early years to recall that solutions were taught to them but without any encouragement to claim ownership of them.

"Share with your sister."

"Quit being a grouch."

"Make sure you're prompt."

"Show respect to your elders."

Children are hardly lacking in directions for the many problems of the day. In fact, most will say they feel overloaded with orders.

But how much time was given to contemplate the philosophies underlying those instructions? You may chuckle at the thought that no parent has the time to talk about heavy-duty philosophies with their young. But it can be done, with real success.

Consider a common scenario in most families. A nine-year-old girl comes to Mom full of frustration because of a dispute with a neighbor. "I hate Susie," she says. "Every time I start talking with one of my friends she gets jealous and won't leave me alone. She thinks she has to be everyone's boss." Familiar enough? Now most moms will respond with something like this: "You shouldn't hate anyone. If you can't get along with Susie any better than that, just leave her alone and play with someone else." The child has an emotional problem; the parent has a ready solution.

But let's look at the approach that encourages contemplative thinking. Mom can respond: "Sounds like you feel disrespected by Susie. No wonder it leaves you feeling angry. What are your options so you won't stay mad the rest of the afternoon?" Most nine-year-olds will not be extremely proficient in arriving at the best options, so you can help: "There's always the choice to hit her. Or you can hold a grudge against her. Or you could choose to play with someone else. Which option makes the most sense to you?"

I am under no illusion that a single conversation like this will produce perfect results each time. Children do not grasp concepts about deep issues in one sitting. But I do know that when parents spend years talking with children about personal issues, a habit can grow. They can think, *What are my options?* or, *Why am I feeling as I do?* As the child grows older, parents can directly introduce abstract notions to the child. For example, to the sixteen-year-old girl feeling insecure about boyfriend problems, the parent can respond, "You've heard that your security is anchored in the Lord; how would it apply to this situation?"

Even if you did not receive encouragement in your childhood to contemplate the meaning and direction of your emotions, you can begin today. For example, suppose you are anxious because a friend is very judgmental and you feel you must only say the "correct" things when in her presence. You do not desire that anxiety, but it is present nonetheless. Contemplate the emotion. Why is it there? Are you afraid of judgments? Have you done anything wrong? Do you have a history that emphasizes proper performances, even at the expense of emotional honesty? What alternatives do you have to the anxiety? How would you communicate differently? Is this judgmental person someone whose approval you truly must have?

By contemplating the meaning and options regarding your emotions, you are assuming that you do in fact have the competence to manage undesirable circumstances. It may require careful thought as you implement that competence, but it *does* exist.

In the last chapter we examined how worth is God-given. We can say the same about personal competence. It is inaccurate for any normal-minded person to say, "I *can't* handle my emotions." You can. Though your mother or father may not have trained you to think so, it is true nonetheless.

I broached this subject with thirty-six-year-old Lisa. She had grown up in an autocratic home where the father ruled the roost. "What I say is what you will do" could have been his motto. He was very opinionated and expected the family to fall into line. Lisa's mother was of a nonconfrontational temperament. She always yielded to her husband's strong will, and she consistently encouraged Lisa to do the same. "Don't upset your father," she would instruct. "You'll be better off in the long run if you don't make waves."

Lisa sought counseling because of recurring depression. In our early sessions we had discussed how depression was related to her anger and inferiority and fear. She had readily grasped these ideas and felt she was gaining an understanding of the many facets of her depression. Though her father had died, she had a husband, Jerry, who was not sensitive to her unique perceptions and tried to cram her into his manner of being.

The major problem confronting Lisa's efforts to change was not her insight. She was quite intelligent and caught on to concepts well. Rather, she had a deep feeling that no matter how much wisdom she might attain, it would ultimately do no good because she had no confidence that she could succeed at being different. "If I am more open regarding my fears or frustrations, as you have suggested," she would say, "Jerry would blow a fuse and I'd be just as miserable as I have always been."

Notice how her sense of incompetence was causing Lisa to collapse. She was assuming that she would not be able to share her feelings in a healthy, productive manner. She feared that her self-revelations would sound wrong or maybe selfish. She assumed that once she shared herself with Jerry, she would collapse if he did not respond well. Though she did not verbalize the words, her suppression of emotions said, "I don't have what it takes to relate properly."

I addressed this issue with her. "Lisa, you're very hard on yourself. I understand that you'll need some delicacy and diplomacy as you become more honest with your husband. What I don't understand is why you assume that it will surely be inappropriate if you expose your inner self. You really beat yourself up!"

A surprised look came to her face. "You seem to insinuate that you're not that worried about how I would communicate. This may seem unreal to you, but I've never really thought of myself as one who had great communication skills. That's never been my forte."

"Just as you might struggle a bit as you learn any new skill, I'd not be surprised if you have a few rough edges as you begin changing your manner of communicating emotions," I replied. "But it seems clear to me that you have solid social skills. You're not an insensitive person. Your needs and feelings are legitimate. So let's ease off the thoughts anchored in defeatism. You've got decent skills—use them."

Many times we lie to ourselves
about what is churning inside.

In her childhood Lisa had been trained to defer to her father's overbearing ways. Her mother modeled how to let someone else call the shots for her. Now as an adult, Lisa had continued this pattern of disbelieving in the validity of her own ideas, and consequently she experienced the emotions of the sin nature more powerfully than necessary.

When we acquiesce to the mind-set of trained incompetence, as Lisa did, we are in direct contradiction of Scripture. The apostle Paul, writing to the Philippians, said, "I can do all things through Him who strengthens me" (4:13). Because we know that Paul had been reared in a legalistic, performance-oriented home, it would be safe to assume that he had not been encouraged as a lad to contemplate the meaning of emotions or the direction of his relationships. We can assume, though, that he had large doses of instruction regarding the external solutions for these same issues. Yet after encountering Christ he concluded what should be true for each of us: "Being personable and managing delicate emotions may not be natural for me, but with God's help I can make adjustments." He believed in his competence, not based on his own capability, but on God's willingness to guide him toward healthiness.

STEPS TOWARD OVERCOMING TRAINED INCOMPETENCE

As you seek to minimize the effects of trained incompetence upon your emotional disposition, you can take some specific steps:

1. *Be willing to acknowledge to yourself what you feel.* As simple as this may seem, it is not. Many times we lie to ourselves about what is churning inside. For instance, an inse-

cure person may have tight defensiveness, yet proclaim, "I like the way I handle stress." Or an angry person may say, "I'm not upset, but I do wish things would be different." Be willing to put your emotions on the line with proper identification.

2. *Determine the meaning or origin of your emotions.* If you are jealous because of your wife's close relationship with a friend, it may be because of a history of being ignored by people you desired to be close to. If you cannot get beyond a depressed mood, it may be because you have always had a tendency to let others dictate your level of worth. Know why you feel the way you do—and be honest.

3. *Put your competent choices into play, even if you meet resistance.* You may decide that, rather than acting on unwarranted fears, you will speak decisively regarding a matter. It could be that you will choose to respond calmly in the face of someone else's rage. Or perhaps you will sidestep false guilt by responding to others with calm confidence. Whatever the choice, you can determine that your manner of handling emotions will be inwardly determined rather than outwardly dictated. If others do not like your choices, you will want to be open-minded enough to hear their feedback. Yet ultimately you will be committed to taking acts of initiative toward personal healthiness.

Your ability to act with emotional strength is made easier if you have a history of relationships that offered encouragement and self-awareness. But even if you did not have such a past, you can determine that today will mark the day you choose to rest in God's promise that He will strengthen you.

As I related these ideas with Lisa, I asked her to make mental notes of the times she flung herself into emotional despair with the use of that one word "can't." She later told me: "Until we discussed my history of learned incompetence, I never realized how often I had bought into the idea of my inadequacy. As a girl I used to be angry that my parents would not let me think more on my own. But now that I'm an adult and I have the chance to be who I am, I have remained stuck in the notion that I cannot do what I really *can* do.

"It's like your parents are still hovering over you telling you how incapable you are. I'd say it's time to move on to a new way of thought."

As adults we each have reached an age of accountability. No longer can we justify our irresponsible emotional habits by saying that others did it to us. By choosing contemplative thinking over old patterns of trained incompetence, we step forward and say, "By the grace of God I will choose appropriateness."

6

THE BARRIER OF EVALUATION EMPHASIS

At the end of second grade my teacher, Miss Taylor, called me to her desk for a private conversation. "Leslie, we're going to be giving out scholarship awards next week, and I thought you'd be interested in seeing your grades at this point." She placed a ruler beneath my name in the grade book to show me a row of A's, with the exception of one B. I nodded my head quietly and took my seat.

Later that day I approached my mother. "Miss Taylor called me to her desk today to let me know I didn't qualify for the scholarship awards. I made a B earlier this year." I was really dejected. The following week when my name was called to receive a certificate at the ceremony, I was stunned. "Surely some mistake has been made," I thought. I reluctantly stepped forward to receive my reward. But, being a kid of integrity, I determined that I could return it to the teacher at the first opportunity.

Have you ever felt confused about your evaluative standing before others? I hope I'm not alone in this regard. We all know what it is like to be under the scrutiny of those who will grade us, and we allow our emotions to fluctuate depending on the outcome. For many of us this tendency is a very conscious

matter. For some it is subconscious. We can each be susceptible to a performance based self-image.

A third major barrier to emotional composure is *evaluation emphasis,* typified by the push to achieve and perform for
self-esteem. The evaluation emphasis places great importance
on a person's comparative standing in various measures of
worth. It is revealed by such thoughts as, *How am I doing now?*
or, *I hope that person will be pleased with me*, or, *What will it
take to keep that guy from criticizing me?*

Beginning in earliest childhood we learn to take stock of
others' judgments. A child's simplest performances or expressions are inevitably met with a grade. Notice the evaluations in
the following scenarios:

- An elementary school girl shows to her dad a picture she has
  drawn. He smiles and says, "This looks terrific! You're an excellent artist."
- A boy hits a home run in a Little League baseball game. On
  the sidelines the coach says, "That was great! Keep up the
  good work."
- A fifth grader brings home an A on a math test. The parent
  replies, "Now that is what I like to see! I'm proud of you."
- A high school student is elected class officer, to which his
  peers reply, "Man, you're lucky! I wish I could have been
  elected to an office."
- A son expresses strong frustration regarding his kid brother's
  annoying behavior. The parent responds to him with the
  comment, "I don't know what's gotten into you, but you cannot continue being such a foul influence."
- A young boy memorizes more Bible verses than anyone else
  in his Sunday school class. The teacher speaks to the entire
  class: "I wish you could each be as responsible as Johnny."

At first glance these statements seem very normal and in-
nocent. A performance of some sort is made and an evaluation
is rendered. Seems innocuous enough, right? Wrong.

As you examine each illustration you will notice that the evaluation, no matter how positive-sounding, carries an implied threat. Each statement telling the child how excellent or exemplary he is has a hidden message: "You must continue to perform up to this high standard or I'll be forced to tell you how bad you are." Logic tells the child that if an excellent performance carries a high mark, a substandard performance necessitates a devaluation.

At a very early age children learn to posture themselves for good grades and to avoid bad grades like the plague. They hesitate to let human frailties be seen because of the certain scorn it will bring. Think back to your own childhood. When you experimented in a behavior your parents would disdain, what did you do? You certainly did not march up to them with full disclosure and report your activities. Why? You knew you would receive an unfavorable evaluation. Or when you felt less than adequate in maintaining certain skills, how did you present yourself to your peers? You avoided talking about the subject or you steered conversations to friendlier topics. If you felt insecure in the presence of someone of the opposite gender, what did you do? You played a game of pretense, attempting to prove that you were beyond the weaknesses of normal people.

This concern about evaluations does not cease once we enter the adult years. The subjects of attention may change, but our posturing for good grades continues. Notice the evaluation concerns in the following examples:

- A salesman has trouble meeting his monthly quota, but when a friend asks about his business the reply is, "I'd say things are going well. I'm doing just fine."
- A couple is having strains in their marriage, but they will never let people know of it because it would draw judgment or alienation.
- A single woman frets over what she will wear for the evening. She must make a good impression.

✔ As a woman looks back upon her youthful days of promiscuity, she wonders if she can ever face the people who know about her embarrassing sins.

✔ At home a man has a habit of temperamental flare-ups, but in public he goes overboard to project a positive image.

The evaluation emphasis is with us in virtually every element of living. We are graded for our achievements, religious fervor, emotional status, external appearance, financial stability, social skills, intellectual prowess, and much more. It is impossible to escape the scrutiny of others.

The more extensive the evaluation emphasis is in our lives, the more we struggle with the emotions produced by the sin nature. Our emotional composure lessens.

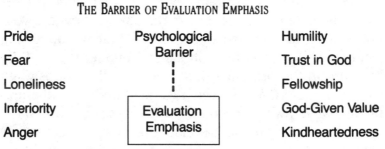

THE BARRIER OF EVALUATION EMPHASIS

Pride	Psychological Barrier	Humility
Fear		Trust in God
Loneliness		Fellowship
Inferiority	Evaluation Emphasis	God-Given Value
Anger		Kindheartedness

Figure 6-1

When our focus is on the judgment of humans, we are detracted from implementing the wholeness and stability that is offered by God. A person with this history of a performance based self-image may audibly hear the concepts associated with the abundant Christian life, but they are rendered void. As ongoing energy is expended to maintain the desired grade, spiritual maturity (and thus emotional stability) is hindered.

Pride: The evaluation emphasis causes persons to be too image conscious. While it is healthy to maintain a positive pride associated with good works, too much performance orientation creates a selfish pride. An overly conscientious nature develops. Efforts are made to put oneself in the best possible light, meaning we attempt to control the way people think about us. Rather than being God-focused we are increasingly self-focused.

Fear: As we are aware of the potential for judgment, fear increases. Though we may skillfully mask those fears in public, inwardly we think, *Can I trust the thoughts others will have about me?* As a result, our defenses become increasingly prominent. When there is a chance for evaluation, we posture ourselves so that weaknesses will be minimized, strengths optimized. The net result is phoniness. Then, when acceptance does come our way, we become vulnerable to doubt: *What if they knew all my flaws?*

---

*Deep down we all resent having
to perform for acceptance.*

Loneliness: Since the evaluation emphasis causes us to present ourselves in measured ways, full connectedness cannot occur in relationships. As we are consumed with performance standings, we create gaps in our relational patterns. Usually this means that persons will gladly share the positive elements of their personalities, but not the negative. Normal struggles regarding insecurities or moral weaknesses are kept secret. True cohesion in relationships is found as persons expose the full extent of their humanness, something toward which performance-oriented persons are disinclined.

Inferiority: When there is a strong emphasis on making the grade, the problem of inferiority is greatly exaggerated. People can become so conscientious about their weaknesses that they succumb too easily to false guilt or feelings of unworthiness or unnecessary apologies. On the other extreme, persons concerned with evaluations will expend extra efforts to create false impressions of superiority. They may attempt to prove themselves by gaining superficial standards for success (such as creating an image anchored in fine clothes, cars, and so on). Or they may succumb to perfectionism, which is an attempt to prove that they are beyond lowly grades.

Anger: Deep down we all resent having to perform for acceptance. So it is only natural that people playing into evaluations will find regular frustration. They may feel anger because others will not give them the respect that should come with good performances. Or perhaps they are easily angered when others do not measure up to their own standards of achievement. Examples would include parents who are too agitated at their kids' subpar qualities and spouses who criticize each other for common humanness.

When I counsel people for emotional difficulties, I usually find that many can recall histories where their self-image was closely linked to externals. One such person was Arthur, who told me, "I always knew my parents loved me, but I also felt I'd better maintain the highest standards in order to keep them happy."

"There is nothing wrong with having high standards," I responded. "How is it that this fed negative emotions?"

"Well, in most respects I could perform well, but there was always this nagging doubt that I should be a notch higher than I really was. For example, I was pretty good at sports, but I wished I could be the star athlete. Or I made mostly A's at school, but I'd never let anyone know when I made a C. The adults at church thought I was a good Christian kid, but that set me up to be devious if I ever did something out of bounds."

"So, in other words, your need to perform for acceptance caused you to feel guarded and less than secure."

"Right. I felt confident as long as the compliments came pouring in. But I simply didn't know what to do when my character flaws might be exposed or if people knew my real inadequacies."

Arthur's struggle is not unlike most of the rest of us. Few developing children have had the luxury of living in an atmosphere of true acceptance, regardless of the performance.

Some people can tell far more severe tales of rejection or abuse that came from the hand of authorities whose standards were terribly selfish or humanly impossible to attain. The effects of this pattern can be debilitating unless a better alternative is learned.

JUDGE NOT

One of the earliest concepts we learn in our Christian walk is the concept of nonjudgment. You were probably young in your relationship with God when you first heard the words, "Judge not, lest you also be judged." Part of the great Sermon on the Mount, Jesus had exposed the fact that we each are infested with sin, thereby rendering us unqualified to judge.

Even in the face of great failure
and disappointment, love can abound.

To illustrate, He said that if we had lust in our hearts, we were equivalent to adulterers; if we hated anyone, we were equivalent to murderers. It was His way of communicating, "Maybe you think you have a higher evaluative standing than others because you have not committed the same open sins that they have. Please get honest. Though you may have decent performances on the outside, inwardly you struggle like everyone else." It is this reality that led to the conclusion, "Don't judge."

Human evaluations are empty. In God's eternal economy they carry absolutely no weight. God and God alone has the right to pass judgment. The apostle Paul reflected this idea in 2 Corinthians 10:12: "For we are not bold to class or compare ourselves with some of those who commend themselves; but when they measure themselves by themselves, and compare themselves with themselves, they are without understanding." Comparative, evaluative thinking shows a lack of spiritual discernment.

This concept of nonjudgment has major implications for healthy living. For example, while parents will still want to spur their children toward excellence, it would best be done with an understanding that excellence is not a prerequisite for love. Even in the face of great failure and disappointment, love can abound. Likewise, in adult relationships (marriage, friendships, fellow workers), high standards and goals can be maintained, but not at the expense of understanding or respect.

When I talked with Arthur about the possibility of restructuring his thinking to eliminate performance criteria for acceptance, his response was, "I don't know if that could realistically be done."

Smiling I responded, "I wish I could tell you that I have personally eliminated all concerns about grading others or receiving their good evaluations. But that is not the case. So I understand your lament. In reality, evaluations and judgments are here to stay. But I am suggesting that we can aim toward the loftier goal of setting aside our worries about performances to the extent that we do not unnecessarily feed painful emotions."

"I'm just thinking how my life might have been different," he reflected, "if my childhood had less emphasis on evaluations. I'd probably have been much more at ease with myself, and I know I'd have been more honest. I wouldn't have worried about playing games of pretense."

"Arthur, even though your childhood did propel you toward a mind-set of evaluation, it's not too late to change. I'd like for you to consider what would be different now if you set those worries aside."

When I talk with people like Arthur, I prompt them to identify how their emotions are ignited by judgmental concerns, then I encourage them to envision their responses that would reflect a different mind-set altogether. Following are some examples of what could be altered:

• A businessman lives under constant scrutiny by a critical manager. Rather than living in high anxiety or anger, he determines that this manager is not God, meaning he will do the best he can without handing over the reins of his emotions to this critic.

- A wife knows that her husband evaluates her worth on the basis of her household performances. She concludes that he would be judgmental no matter who he was married to. So she decides to handle her responsibilities as best she can, without unnecessarily catering to his impetuous ways or defending herself when in fact there is no need for defense.

- A student realizes that he is in school to learn ideas and concepts, not just to make grades. He pursues his studies with the primary goal of self-improvement.

- A Christian recognizes that human perfection is an illusion. While he deeply respects God's perfect and lofty standards, he refuses to flog himself each time sin occurs. He is determined to learn from his errors while also accepting himself as he grows.

Even when this mind-set of nonjudgment is not trained in the developmental years, it can be learned in the adult years as our minds are yielded to truths from God's word.

DESCRIPTIVE THINKING

At this point you maybe be wondering, "If I let go of the evaluation emphasis, what will I replace it with?" The alternative for evaluative emphasis is *descriptive thinking.*

OVERCOMING EVALUATION EMPHASIS

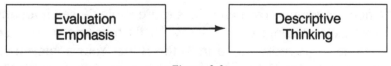

Figure 6-2

Descriptive thinking is characterized by a willingness to openly appraise performances or events without a judgmental attitude. It recognizes good versus bad, excellent versus mediocre, yet it is guided by the understanding that performances and achievements stand separate from human worthiness. As such, descriptive thinking can create a milieu that still encourages good performance, yet emphasizes acceptance. Note in the following examples how the scenarios presented earlier in this chapter are guided by descriptive thinking:

- A grade school girl shows a picture she has drawn to her dad. He says: "This looks like a springtime day. I see a house with an apple tree to the side. The sun is shining and birds are flying in the distance. You must have enjoyed making this drawing!"
- A boy hits a home run in a Little League game, to which the coach exclaims, "Man, as you were rounding the bases you were running as fast as your legs could carry you. What excitement! There's nothing quite like the thrill of a home run!"
- When a fifth grade student brings home an A on a math test, the parent says, "I know you were happy when you saw that big A on the top of the page. Looks like you had those problems figured out."
- When a high school student is elected class officer, a friend could remark, "It's really gratifying, isn't it, to know that your friends put confidence in you like that."
- A son expresses frustration regarding his brother's annoying behavior, to which the parent replies, "It's times like this when you don't know exactly what to say or do. I guess this shows that it will require some thought as you try to play the role of peacemaker."
- When the young boy memorizes more Bible verses than anyone else, the teacher could say, "This tells me that you're wanting to be more tuned in to the Bible. Your achievement shows that a lot of time and effort was spent last week on this project."

Do you notice the major difference between descriptive thinking and the evaluation emphasis? When descriptions are spoken, we no longer speak exclusively about external matters, but to the internal parts of the person. Feelings or unique efforts or motivations are acknowledged. The person, not the achievement, is center stage.

In addition, descriptive thinking carries no threat. While evaluations cause individuals to wonder about how they would be received in the event of failure, descriptions allow us to continue talking about the inner person in the midst of that failure. Genuineness can be encouraged. Worth does not rise or fall with the latest event. Security is experienced. Yet encouragement to produce good results can still be offered.

The implications for descriptive thinking in the lives of adults are enormous:

- The person feeling guilty for past sins can honestly describe how right living could be found with specific adjustments, yet the guilt will not linger unnecessarily as that person sidesteps harsh self-criticism.
- Even as individuals attempt to maintain honorable standards, they will not be weighted down by self-imposed perfectionism.
- Relationships will become more meaningful as personal feelings and perceptions are exposed and discussed.
- Not consumed with worries about judgment, concepts like grace and forgiveness can be incorporated in the mind.
- Status symbols and other superficial distinctions are set aside, allowing people to enjoy each other for what they are.

Arthur grinned as we discussed exchanging his evaluations for descriptions. "Do you realize how different I will be among family and acquaintances when I begin speaking in this fashion? People will think something strange is happening to me." We both chuckled.

"I guess you will develop a reputation different from what you've had before, but I'm assuming it will be a change that will pay rewarding dividends."

"Just thinking about being descriptive, I can imagine how the little events of the day will be processed differently. For instance, if my wife tells me about a project she completed at her job, I can comment on her feelings of accomplishment rather than on the job itself."

"My hope, Arthur, is that you will be more tuned to the person and that your rapport with your wife will deepen."

"I have a question for you, though," he said. "I'm committed to speak with fewer evaluations, but it's quite predictable that virtually everyone else in my world will continue focusing on outer performances. How am I supposed to respond to their ongoing tendency to grade me?"

"I wish I could say that you are wrong in your assumption, but you're right on target," I replied. "Why don't we make an allowance for others to continue in their evaluations of you, with the understanding that you are under no obligation to conform your lifestyle to their judgments?"

Perhaps the greatest frustration for a person who is choosing a healthier pattern of living is the insistence of other people to continue in the ways of relating that feed painful emotions. But since we are powerless to change others, we can only choose to disassociate from their mannerisms to the extent that we exercise responsible autonomy. That requires an awareness of the moments when others "invite" us into maladaptive patterns.

Ultimately, descriptive persons
are enacting humility.

Arthur, for instance, was more inclined to think about improving his relational and spiritual life than was his wife, Evelyn. She professed to be too busy to concern herself with thoughts about personality or relationship philosophies. "If you feel the need to get counseling and read your books," she would say, "that's your business. But don't expect me to do the same. That's not my cup of tea."

Likewise, Arthur had attempted on several occasions to talk with his elderly parents about relating differently, but they too were unreceptive to his efforts. He once told me, "I'm a forty-year-old man, but my folks still have performance requirements before they'll give me a pat on the back."

We decided that if he wanted, he could twist his family's arms until they understood the insights he was learning. But common sense told us that would only create more problems than it would solve. So Arthur determined that whenever his wife or parents judged him, it was their prerogative. But he was under no obligation to alter his personality to fit their judgments. He would still seek to be pleasant and cooperative, but he would do so because of choice, not fear.

Arthur gave an illustration of how this affected a particular incident at home. One Saturday he had more yard work than normal, and in the process of doing his chores he forgot to do his wife a favor he had promised. She became angry, fussed at him, then did not speak for several hours. "She was judging me because my performance was not up to par. But I chose to side-step her hooks. Being descriptive, I told myself that I had in fact disappointed her. But then I also recognized that she was out of line to consider me a bad husband for a common mistake. Rather than becoming angry at her evaluation of me, I vowed to do a better job of remembering my promises. But I also gave myself permission to allow for imperfection along the way."

The evaluation emphasis tends to turn humans into machines, whereas descriptive thinking lets humans be human. Excellence can still be pursued by those who sidestep evaluations, but it is not done with the intent of impressing others. Instead, the motivation is pure desire.

Ultimately, descriptive persons are enacting humility. It is a matter of arrogant pride for any person to assume the capacity to judge another. Humility, which is anchored in a modest self-appraisal, recognizes that whereas God grants people positions of authority and He encourages us to exhort and stimulate each other, we have no position that allows us to hold ourselves above others.

Realism reminds us that evaluations are here to stay. For instance, when I speak publicly someone may say to me afterward, "You did a good job." At that moment I remind myself, *I did not come here to receive a report card. There's always the possibility someone else evaluated me quite differently.* I would prefer to hear more descriptive words like, "Dr. Carter, when you spoke about handling anger, it really hit home in my life; I've got some ideas about how to adjust." Nonetheless, I allow for the fact that I will be judged no matter how strongly I would prefer simple descriptions.

7

THE BARRIER OF IMPERATIVE THINKING

Where were you on July 4, 1986? Perhaps I can jog your memory by reminding you that this date marked the centennial celebration of the Statue of Liberty. The event was made more prominent by the fact that in 1976, when we celebrated the bicentennial of the Declaration of Independence, America was in its malaise, still reeling from the aftereffects of Vietnam and Watergate. The 1986 celebration, by contrast, came during a time of national optimism and rejuvenation.

I remember the upbeat mood that day as we gathered with my extended family, watching on television the festivities in New York harbor. More than twenty thousand boats jammed the waters. Among them were twenty-two tall ships from eighteen countries. Six million people were in attendance, each electrified with anticipation. President Reagan, the great communicator himself, gave one of his most inspiring speeches extolling the virtues of liberty, reminding Americans of our great heritage and our responsibilities to uphold freedom worldwide.

Then the fireworks began. They were unlike any before. All the stops were pulled. With Lady Liberty as the backdrop, the skies were a perpetual kaleidoscope of color. Each explosion was carefully synchronized with the familiar patriotic songs. The most hair-raising moment came during the fire-works' grand finale when Christian artist Sandi Patti performed her rendition of "The Star Spangled Banner," churning the audience into incredible euphoria. Never had I heard such music! Macho man that I am, I fought to hold back the tears as I sat in the midst of my family, but the lump in my throat was the size of a grapefruit. I could only think, *Thank God I live in the country that is the standard bearer for freedom!*

We love to celebrate freedom. Ask virtually any person on the street what they like about America, and you will hear plaudits regarding the privilege to be free. But as I talk with people in the counseling office, I find that a great number of them feel anything but free. When they tell me of their depression or anxiety or anger or guilt, they relate how oppressed they feel. Most will reveal how they attempt to manage problems with spouses or parents or co-workers who are controlling to the point of being dictatorial. They complain that the lack of freedom inhibits emotional stability.

IMPERATIVE THINKERS

A man once came to my office who told me that he had uncompromising principles. Then he quickly added that he had experienced defeat in virtually all his close relationships. "My problem," he said, "is that I'm so right I'm wrong." I thought for a moment and inwardly concluded that I could relate to him. I've been there myself. It is possible to have very powerful notions of correctness that give "permission" to condemn, reject, and criticize.

Many people who remain stuck in the emotions produced by sin have been overexposed to the problem of *imperative thinking*. This is characterized by a tendency to adhere to powerful opinions and expectations to the extent that correctness becomes more important than acceptance.

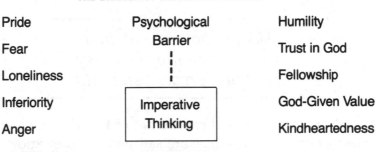

Figure 7-1

Imperative thinking is very directive, or black and white. It is guided by the assumption that life can and should fit into a specific order; therefore great efforts are made to coerce correctness. To identify this pattern of thought, watch for certain key words: *have to, must, can't, should, ought to, supposed to, had better, got to, need to*. These words imply, "Get into the proper mold and do not stray."

Think back to your childhood to determine if you were ever exposed to imperative thinking. In truth, we each have experienced this; the differences among us are a matter of degree. For example, you were probably told that you were *supposed to* get along with your cousins. You have *got to* clean your room before supper. You *had better* not say naughty words. And so on. Perhaps the imperative atmosphere was strong enough that the imperative words did not have to actually be spoken. A parent may have simply given you a look ("The Look"), which created great fear indeed.

Imperative thinking, though, is not confined merely to childhood experiences. Husbands and wives, for instance, may have a long list regarding the ways each other should act, speak, or feel. Employers may be heavy-handed in the way they treat employees. Peer groups may have unspoken, yet firm, standards that must be maintained if the relationships can survive. Churches may impose unbending dogma on their members.

Most people are at their worst when they feel they must fit a prescribed mold.

People in our world can be full of knowledge regarding correct living, and, once they are satisfied that they know what is right, they feel fully comfortable in imposing that correctness on others. What is worse, once you have been exposed to imperative thinking, you may then choose to respond with your own imperative agenda, thereby throwing fuel on the fire.

Although it is good, even necessary, to have well-established ideas of right and wrong, it is difficult for most of us to maintain emotional composure when it is taken too far. We become impatient and irritable. We experience tightness in our stomachs. We criticize and judge. We sulk. We retreat behind walls of deceit. It is an exception to the rule to have balanced emotions when imperative thinking is strongly present. Most people are at their worst when they feel they must fit a prescribed mold.

Note in the following examples how imperative thinking hinders emotional balance:

- A father thinks his children *had better* be respectful and becomes very impatient when they act otherwise.
- A marriage partner knows how the spouse is *supposed to* communicate and becomes critical and bitter when discussions are nonproductive.
- A mother tells her children they *had better* listen to her and loses her cool when they are distracted.
- A school teacher knows how her schedule *must* unfold and feels defeated at the end of the day when nothing went as planned.

✓ A driver knows what courtesy *should* be extended to him on the freeway and becomes tense as other drivers are careless.

Do you see the trend in these simple scenarios? Correctness is given priority over kindness. Performances are more important than relationships. Obligation is emphasized over choice. Love is smothered by rules.

Some will promote imperative living by saying, "But I insist on having order." When they do this, they misunderstand a key ingredient of communication—covert messages. When someone communicates imperatives to you, notice the silent but powerful messages they imply:

- "I'll not accept you until you meet my conditions for acceptance."
- "I have little trust for you. You probably will make poor decisions."
- "I'm superior to you; keep that in mind as we relate."
- "You are obliged to fit my mold, be under my control."

It is because of these covert messages that people respond poorly to imperative thinking. Emotions become erratic. Notice how imperative thinking increases the tendency toward the five negative emotions produced by sin.

Pride: Imperative thinking is the language of pride. Arrogance is intact as imperative people believe they can actually do the thinking on behalf of others. God's first restriction to Adam was to refrain from the Tree of the Knowledge of Good and Evil. That is, let God be the final arbitrator of ultimate right and wrong. Imperative people, though, have determined to ignore this instruction, elevating self to a god-like place of authority. Being dictatorial and condescending, they exhibit a self-absorption. The world is required to revolve around *their* preferences.

Fear: Imperative thinking reflects fear and produces fear. The more controlling a person acts, the more it implies a lack of trust. By attempting to keep a tight lid on performances, emotions, and so on, imperative people show an insecurity regarding their ability to handle differentness. When others encounter imperatives, they usually respond with defensiveness. This relational style of control does nothing to encourage openness but, instead, causes people to feel inhibited and guarded. Phoniness increases as games of "cat and mouse" become prominent.

Loneliness: Imperative thinking does nothing to foster relationship cohesion. Instead, it drives a wedge between relationships. Personal matters such as feelings or unique perceptions are discouraged. Machinelike performance is mandated, leaving little room to develop intimacy. For closeness to occur in relationships, openness and vulnerability must be present. Imperative thinking encourages the opposite.

---

*Christians can sometimes
be among the worst abusers
of imperative thinking.*

Inferiority: When people are acting imperatively, they appear to be in a position of superiority when in fact they are attempting to cover any question regarding their inferiority. Imperative thinking persists in the illusion that, if control can be attained, worthiness and stability are found. In fact, imperative thinking produces struggles with chronic false guilt. Acceptance and personal value are only as secure as the latest performance. Unhealthy traits such as perfectionism, workaholism, or even chronic apologizing are fostered.

Anger: Imperative thinking is both a by-product and an instigator of anger. Because imperative people have such rigid requirements for people and circumstances, and because the world is sure not to meet those rigid requirements, irritability and frustration are highly predictable. Imperative thinking perpetuates struggles with impatience, jealousy, envy, fretting. It is difficult, if not impossible, to crave control in an imperfect world and then be satisfied with the results.

In my years of counseling, it has become painfully obvious to me that Christians can sometimes be among the worst abusers of imperative thinking. They can take the teachings of the Bible and use them for the sake of condemnation. Seeing Scripture as the ultimate list of rules, they heap upon themselves or others psychological and emotional problems never intended by God.

One example of this is illustrated by a man named Neal. In his early forties, he experienced great frustration in his relationship with his father, who had always been overbearing. "My dad is a pillar of the community," he told me. "Everywhere he goes he commands respect. There is a certain aura about him that implies strength."

He told me, though, that he had never gotten along with his father because of his need to control. "Whatever I do is not up to his standards. He has precise ideas about how I should be rearing my two sons. He gives me advice regarding career decisions, even though I don't ask for it. When we go out to eat, he has to have everything his way. He knows no compromise. I want to avoid any contact with him, but I can't because, after all, he is my father."

"Could I assume that you've contended with your father like this for a long time?"

"All my life. When I was young, he was good about attending my sports activities. But even so, I stayed angry because he wanted to call the shots regarding most of my personal decisions. He told me who I could socialize with. He would correct my grammar or tell me how to improve my sports skills. It's like I was never given permission to think for myself. Dad has always had to be in control."

After forty years of exposure to this imperative mind-set, Neal had responded to his father with his own brand of imperatives. He would say things such as, "Dad has *got to* get off my back," or, "He *can't* go on being so critical," or, "He *should* take more interest in my sons' activities." Rather than choosing to go a different route, Neal complained about his father's mannerisms, but in many respects he was a carbon copy of him.

Adding to the tension, many of Neal's imperatives—and those of his father—were "biblically based." For example, each could justify his stubbornness by saying something like, "The Bible says you ought to . . ." or, "If we're going to be a Christian family, we'll have to . . ."

ALLOWING FOR FREEDOM

Neal and his father are a classic example of how imperative thinking can become so lodged in people's minds that relational success is nearly impossible. If the bondage of imperative thinking is to be broken, a new system of thinking will need to be invoked. That thought system will be anchored in a mind of *freedom.*

Freedom is not defined as irresponsibility or chaos or flippancy. Rather, *freedom* is defined as the presence of choices. In the very first sentence spoken to Adam, God introduced this idea when He instructed, "From the fruit of the trees of the garden you may eat freely." He intended for all people to live with an abundance of choices. Then God added: "But from the tree of the knowledge of good and evil you shall not eat" (Genesis 2:16–17). Specifically, He meant that no human has the wisdom to hold ultimate knowledge of right and wrong. That wisdom is reserved for God alone. (This is something imperative people ignore).

OVERCOMING IMPERATIVE THINKING

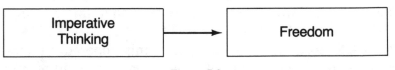

Figure 7-2

So each person is free to choose how to feel, think, speak, act. But a wise person will also acknowledge that this freedom is best used when considering God's ways first. We do not have to submit to God, as Adam clearly proved, but we find the most positive consequences when we freely choose to do so.

Understanding the God-given privilege of freedom, we can make several assumptions as we try to break the hold of imperative thinking on our lives:

- No human has the prerogative to control another. Therefore, if someone attempts to control me, I am under no obligation to mechanically comply.
- Each human has permission to choose how he will approach life. This is an issue between himself and God.
- Freedom can produce a depth of thinking that will never accompany imperatives. It forces a person to ask "why" questions.
- Each individual is responsible for the direction of his or her own life. Consequences and rewards will be factored into choices.
- Desire rather than duty will become the primary motivator for behavior.

Some people will balk when they are encouraged toward freedom. They may ask, "Wouldn't this lead to an anything-goes way of life?" The answer is, "It might." Whereas freedom can feel refreshing, it is also risky. In freedom a spouse could choose to be unresponsive. A child might choose disrespect. A Christian could choose carnality. A worker might choose laziness. These are all possibilities. When mankind fell into sin, God did not remove freedom. He fully knew that it could be abused.

A lack of freedom, however, leads to worse results. We lose our humanness, becoming robotic instead. So in spite of the risk, God chose to retain freedom even after sin. He did implement a system of consequences, however, to promote deep thought about the abuse of freedom. It is in the contemplation of consequences that freedom can be held in proper perspective.

As I spoke with Neal about his tensions with his father, we identified how imperative thinking had been a constant in their relationship. Then I asked him to consider adopting a mind of freedom as a healthier alternative. "I know you are weary of having to guess how you must respond to keep your father pleased. Why not relax and give yourself the permission to be who you are?"

"But wouldn't that be selfish of me?"

"It might, although it doesn't have to be. That's for you to determine. I'm making the assumption that you are quite capable of making your own choices without having to filter them through your father's dictates. What do you think?"

Neal sat quietly for a moment, then replied, "I've been angry for many years that my dad is so overbearing, but it never really occurred to me until right now that I have the freedom to be who I am. I've been so busy protesting his ways that I respond to him just as I don't want him to respond to me."

"So how would freedom make a difference?" I wanted him to see how his emotions were ultimately his own responsibility.

"I guess I could remind myself that I can make the decisions in my life that seem appropriate to me, and if he doesn't agree, then he's free to disagree."

"That would take a lot of pressure off yourself," I responded. "But it might also open a whole new can of worms. He might choose to become even more overbearing. Are you up to the challenge?"

---

*Freedom allows relational
boundaries to exist.*

"It would be very different for me. I'm so used to responding to his potential reaction that I don't really take into account that my emotions are ultimately a matter of my own initiative."

We discussed some potential implications of freedom. We acknowledged that he could actually choose to hold a grudge against his father or behave rudely or ignore him alto-gether. These were real options, although they carried the very real possibility that the relationship could be irrevocably harmed. He also had the choice to speak assertively or behave independently or to accept him as he is.

As Neal reflected on his choices, he stated, "Obviously I want to do what is right and sound. So even though I know I have the option to be unruly, I don't want to go that route. I guess I could learn to be more assertive, particularly in just liv-ing according to my convictions, not his. But I imagine that my best option will be to accept him for what he is."

"I happen to agree with you," I said. "Can you see that this option would be extremely difficult if you did not first have the option not to do it?"

"Yes, I really can see that. I've never quite thought of it like that before, though, because I've always lectured myself about how a Christian is supposed to respond to these kinds of situations. But I was getting to the point of resenting those Christian principles because they seemed so impossible."

Neal was learning that freedom allows relational bound-aries to exist. By being pulled into his father's headstrong ways, he had been taught, "You cannot be separate and distinct. Our family must be completely the same in thought and preference." Paradoxically this insistence upon sameness created aversions, while allowance for difference would lead to harmony.

Imperative thinking is intrusive, whereas freedom refrains from interfering with another's capacity to choose. In freedom, advice can still be offered, suggestions can be made. Yet there is a willing recognition that God made personalities unique.

LAW AND GRACE

Ultimately imperative thinking is a form of legalism. Im-perative people are not so interested in the personal elements of living as they are in maintaining their version of correct dog-ma. The net result is a type of slavery. Either they attempt to enslave others through control and manipulation or they feel enslaved themselves as they grow weary of the burden of always having to be structured.

Grace, on the other hand, gives people room to think. It does not force anyone into a mold, yet it paradoxically creates a stronger, more positive hold on a relationship. Imagine a friend who insists that you must spend time with her. You have to be available when she needs you. You've got to know the right words to say at all times. You cannot afford to make mistakes. Eventually you will grow weary and seek release from that person. But then imagine a friend who loves you for who you are. She clearly stands for what is good, yet never judges when you err. She is patient and resilient. She has no agenda for you. How do you react? If you are like me, you keep going back to that person. Deep bonding occurs.

In the same way, a mind of freedom creates an atmosphere conducive to grace. Grace does not mean that the old law is considered null and void. It is still respected. Grace, however, creates a different type of bonding among people. It is gentle yet powerful. It draws in rather than repulses.

When grace becomes natural to your lifestyle, differences will occur in everyday communications. Note the following examples:

- When you speak with your children, harshness will be removed from your tone of voice. Gentleness can accompany your statements, even in discipline.
- As you openly disagree with a family member or spouse, you can take time to comprehend the other person's perspective, no matter how off-beat it may seem.
- When another person is in a foul mood, it is not your job to talk him out of it. You can respond with patience in spite of the fact that you'd prefer a more pleasant disposition.
- Phoniness and pretense will be absent from your relating style. Authenticity will be the norm.
- You can be known as an accepting person even as you maintain strong opinions of right and wrong.

Two biblical illustrations stand out as representatives of freedom in relating. The first is the story of the prodigal son, recorded in Luke 15:11–32. The father gave him the freedom he wanted, knowing the son would abuse it. But in time, the gift of freedom caused the son to turn around and make healthy choices. The elder brother, representing the imperative mind-set, was not pleased that such a gift would be extended and that the relationship could be restored in spite of the young man's irresponsibilities. Nonetheless, Christ's purpose in this parable was to illustrate how grace, not the law, ultimately would win in relationships.

The second illustration does not have a positive ending. It is the story of the rich young ruler in Matthew 19:16–22. The wealthy man, upon asking Jesus' requirement to enter His kingdom, was told that he needed to shed himself of his love for material possessions. Not liking the Lord's response, he walked away. And though it clearly saddened Jesus to be rejected like this, He did not chase after him with a lecture about how he should have responded. Jesus acknowledged his privilege to choose, even wrongly.

In the same way, we have no guarantees that freedom will produce perfection or godliness. Like the prodigal son, our freedom may lead to some poor choices along the way. Like the encounter with the rich young ruler, we may find that others choose to reject our feelings or ideas. That is a by-product of living in a sin-infested world.

But in spite of freedom's risks, there is no other way to discover godly grace. The emotionally balanced person will be the one who learns to anchor in God's truth while acknowledging the omnipresence of choices. Decisions regarding emotional composure or appropriate behavior will not be dependent upon others' demands. Emotional independence can be found as the mind considers the repercussions of freely selected responses.

- If you handle anger in abrasive ways or in unproductive passivity, it is because you have determined it to be the behavior of choice. Likewise, if you are kind or forgiving, it is not an obligatory act but a preferred option.

- When you are critical, it is because you have chosen to indulge your self-preoccupations. And when you are encouraging, it is caused by a decision to give your relationships a high priority.
- Defensiveness is a matter of the will, just as authenticity is pursued because you desire it over other options.
- You worry because you have chosen it over composure, whereas you can accept unwanted circumstances by choosing to relinquish the tendency to fret.

Many other illustrations could be given to illustrate how we can respond to our world with either imperatives or freedom. Though your history may have given you an inclination toward a controlling mind-set, it is possible to decide that you will filter your thoughts about your circumstances through a mind of freedom.

8

The Barrier of Mythical Thinking

A woman once asked me in all seriousness, "Is there *anyone* who has never struggled with anger or sadness or insecurity?" I responded that no one is immune from such problems. Because we each bear the burden of sin and we each interact with fellow sinners, we are guaranteed to experience some manner of suffering. Count on it.

Her reply reflected a naïveté: "Well, that seems so unfair. It seems to me that with all the knowledge we have these days we should be able to live without having so many strains."

Before dismissing this woman's lament as totally simplistic, recognize that there have probably been times when you have entertained similar thoughts. We each have had moments of fantasy when we indulged thoughts of a more utopian world. A dissatisfied wife has dreamed about having a husband who tends to her emotional needs more sensitively. A businessperson wishes for more autonomy and greater pay, then makes imaginary plans about how the good life would unfold. A student yearns to be free from the headaches of academics. A single person aches for companionship. Not one of us is immune from thoughts that carry us, if only for a few moments, into a dream world where problems are brushed aside and peace and contentment are experienced in abundance.

Whereas it can be normal to have a few such desires, some people cling to their ideals so powerfully that it creates a tendency toward *mythical thinking*. This can be defined as clinging to false hopes as a means of confronting real problems. One easy way to detect the presence of mythical thinking in a person's mind-set is to listen for key phrases indicating an unrealistic view of life:

"I just wish . . ."
"If only you would . . ."
"Why can't you just . . ."
"I can't believe you would . . ."
"Why in the world would . . ."

Each of these statements implies that the person is clinging to a thought pattern that emphasizes a perfect outcome to problems in spite of evidence that the perfection does not and will not exist. Following are some typical examples of how this mythical style of thinking can feed emotional duress:

- A husband is frustrated by his wife's finicky ways. He knows how good relating should unfold, so he deludes himself by thinking that, if he makes the right convincing statement, she will restructure her entire disposition.

- A secretary's boss exhibits an inconsiderate nature. Knowing how inappropriate this is, she and a co-worker whisper their incredulity that anyone would live in such a state of discontentment.

- A minister experiences a bout with depression. He adds to his woes by telling himself that a clergyman should never have such a problem.

- A mother is embarrassed because her two young children are misbehaving in the grocery store line. She tells herself that she can't bear to have others think of her as an incompetent mother, so she reacts by reprimanding them harshly.

Can you detect the mythical thinking in each of these illustrations? In each case a problem occurs that is met with a response driven by idealism. The fantasy of perfection is so strong that it actually causes the person to experience worsened emotions.

At the base of mythical thinking is a desire for pain avoidance. Certainly no one *wants* pain. Given the choice, we would prefer to live with nothing but positives. Or, if we cannot expect positives all the time, we would at least choose not to have ongoing struggles and suffering.

Yet pain exists, sometimes in abundance. The balanced personality still does not relish the pain, yet there is an allowance for it. That does not imply that pain is accepted lightheartedly, for it is not a light subject. It does mean that shock is not registered when pain rears its ugly head.

When mythical thinking is employed, notice how it feeds the five major emotions, thus increasing the pain that we so deeply wish to avoid.

The Barrier of Mythical Thinking

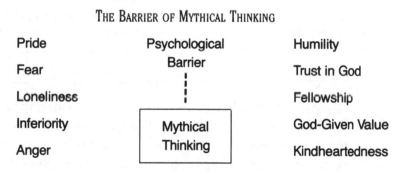

Pride	Psychological	Humility
Fear	Barrier	Trust in God
Loneliness		Fellowship
Inferiority	Mythical	God-Given Value
Anger	Thinking	Kindheartedness

Figure 8-1

Pride: Invariably, the myths we indulge have a self-serving aspect. This is pride, the preoccupation with self. Our fantasies create the desire to have a fully contained world where all the bad can be controlled and the good can be complete. Whereas there is certainly nothing wrong with wanting to have good prevail over bad, problems erupt when we do so to the extent that we maintain a self-preoccupation regarding the things we cannot control.

Fear: Since mythical thinking inhibits our ability to deal with reality, as we nurse such a mind-set we set ourselves up for fear. We become increasingly intimidated by distasteful experiences to the extent that a type of panic occurs. It may at times be normal or necessary to defend ourselves against undesirable input, but mythical thinking causes our defensiveness to be too powerful and impenetrable.

---

*The longer we cling to myths,
the more susceptible we are to
bitterness, resentment, and depression.*

Loneliness: Because mythical thinking is not reality based, it leads to unrealistic interchanges in relationships. For instance, if a person clings to the myth that her marriage should be full of perfect communication, deep isolation and estrangement will be felt when it does not occur. Ultimately, people feel increased isolation because they sense that they have no capacity to connect successfully with others.

Inferiority: The myths we hold are high and lofty—and unattainable. The logical conclusion, then, is that mythical thinking causes persons to assume an inferior status since they do not meet those high goals. As we realize that our myths do not come true, we are prone to feelings of unworthiness. We feel guilty unnecessarily. We may try to find means to compensate for lowliness by overachievement or perfectionism.

Anger: Ultimately, mythical thinking feeds anger. In spite of the impossibility of reaching our ideals, we indulge frustration because we are stuck in ruts we never desired. As we witness how others do not suffer as badly, envy erupts. We become impatient, waiting for problems to just go away. The longer we cling to myths, the more susceptible we are to bitterness, resentment, and depression. Overidealization causes us to grumble that the world is not fair, so we feel justified in holding grudges until justice is served.

WHY MYTHICAL THINKING DEVELOPS

There are two general trends that cause individuals to become caught in the throes of mythical thinking. On one extreme, a person may interpret his past history as so good that he holds the impossible expectation that life owes him a continuation of the same. This can be referred to as a *mind of deservedness.* On the other extreme, a person can have so much suffering or pain that the mind gravitates to a utopian dream world to find images of splendor. There is a desperate hope that one day all the misery can be laid to rest. This would be referred to as a *mind of despair.* Let's look at these separately.

A HISTORY OF DESERVEDNESS

Angie spoke with me about her reason for seeking counseling. In her early thirties, she looked like she could have just stepped out of a fashion catalog. Her blonde hair curled perfectly at the ends, barely touching her shoulders. She wore just the right blend of make-up, not so much to appear gaudy but just enough to look fresh. Her suede leather skirt and silk blouse made the statement, "I always want to look my best." She spoke crisply, not wanting to say anything that sounded too extreme.

"My problem is with anxiety," she explained. "Just a few nights ago I had a terrible panic attack. I became very nervous just about bedtime. My breathing was abrupt, and I thought I was going to suffocate. It was awful." As she spoke red blotches began to cover her neck. She went on to explain in great detail that she was tense much of the time. Her seven-year-old son and four-year-old daughter were on her nerves constantly. They upset her because they just wouldn't mind. "I never acted disrespectfully toward my parents when I was young," she said.

When I asked Angie to tell me about her early family life, she smiled fondly and said, "Oh, my parents were just *perfect*! I can't think of anything negative to tell you about them. I know you'll want to dig up some great childhood trauma, but you'll find that there simply was none." She continued by giving examples of her mother's generous and available spirit and her father's even-handed way of leading the family. As she spoke I became increasingly impressed by her need to overidealize her past. It seemed so unreal.

The better I came to know Angie, the more I realized that she was steeped in mythical thinking because of this past "perfect" history. Her parents had gone overboard to please her and to give her the good life, leaving her unprepared for the harsh realities awaiting her in the adult years. She had lived with the illusion that she would not have to struggle. She had never seen her parents angry, nor did they ever expose insecurities or weaknesses. Angie was compliant, so she just fell in line with their proper ways. But when she got married and had to contend with children who would not obey (really they were just being normal kids) and with a husband who was not as perfect as her father, she began to come apart at the seams. She desperately wanted the utopian life she had known earlier.

When people like Angie expect the wonderful life, they are in for a great disappointment. That is not to say that good relations are impossible. They simply are not going to be perfect. Inconsistency, disappointment, miscommunication, and insensitivity are a certainty. Mythical thinkers will acknowledge that such problems happen to others, but not to them! A mind of deservedness is in place that causes them to think, *I'm not supposed to have the same problems as everyone else. I'm unique.*

A HISTORY OF DESPAIR

Some people arrive at mythical thinking via an entirely different path. Rather than a history of persistent bliss, they recall the opposite. They had times when they felt so bewildered and confused that the only way to defend themselves from pain was to dream of the day that it would all go away.

One such person was Donna. In her mid-forties, she was twice divorced and lived with her only child, a nineteen-year-old daughter. She explained that her daughter was her closest friend. In her most recent divorce settlement she had received enough cash to make it on her own for a while. But she was going to have to eventually get back to work to support her lifestyle. She came to counseling because she was bitter and resentful.

"I can't understand why my husband would want to leave," she said with bewilderment. Though she had jet-black hair, her face bore wrinkles that made her look older than she really was. "I've had a hard life, and he's only made things worse. We were married for twelve years, and I poured myself into our marriage. I gave him the best life he could want. He never lifted a finger at home because I waited on him hand and foot. But the way he showed appreciation was to get a girlfriend fifteen years younger. I can't believe he would stoop to such behavior. Even when I told him I'd take him back, he turned me away. Why couldn't he just receive my love and be satisfied?"

I was hearing those familiar mythical phrases: "I can't believe ... Why couldn't he just ..." I knew she was craving the ideal life that would never be, so I asked her to tell me more about herself.

Donna's early life was not pretty. Her mother had worked many jobs during her childhood, mostly as a waitress. They had moved frequently, and on several occasions she had lived with her grandmother while her mother was off trying to find roots. Several boyfriends and husbands had been in and out of her mother's life. Donna remembered that one of them had been real friendly, but the rest were either disinterested in her or very harsh.

Because of the family instability, Donna had not made close childhood friends. In fact, she spent many hours feeling very isolated, particularly on the weekends and during summer months. As she would while away her time, she was given to dreaming and fantasizing. *One day*, she told herself, *I'm going to get away from this loneliness. I'm going to have a good life.*

At twenty she married a young man on his way toward a medical career. She envisioned how they would have a large house, many friends, a place in the community. But she was unprepared for the reality of her husband's demanding schedule as a student and resident. After nine years of waiting for their glorious life to arrive, she left him, determined to find a man already established who could give her what she needed. Soon after, she met her second husband. And though she was pleased with his large bank account, she was quickly disillusioned by his lack of relational skills.

"I'm giving the marriage 110 percent of my effort. What's wrong with him? Why can't he love me?" She endured his aloofness for years but was miserable because of his complete unwillingness to be open with her.

I expressed empathy with Donna's plight. I told her it was understandable that she would feel hurt. But her disillusionment would override her ability to be consoled when she asked questions such as, "Why did God give me such a lousy life? Why wouldn't He answer my pleas for a husband who would care for me?"

No perfect marriage exists.
All children will disappoint.
Friends will not always be capable
or willing to be fully tuned in.

In reality, no answer to those questions would have suited Donna. Rather than genuinely seeking satisfactory explanations for such hard circumstances, she was indulging the notion that she should be able to find a dream life, taking her away from her lifelong misery. As events became increasingly dissatisfying, she clung the more desperately to the craving for deliverance, unaware that her sense of desperation only made her troublesome emotions more intense.

When people have a history of desperation, they often use the defense mechanism called *reaction formation.* They protect themselves from pain by inventing a world where the opposite—happiness—is the standard. Fearing that they will be doomed with never-ending pain, they nurse their emotional wounds by believing that one day all the hurt will go away. The result is that they eventually overreact to their adult pain, making it more intense than it might be, thereby pushing away the very ones they hope will rescue them.

REPLACING MYTHICAL THINKING WITH TRUTH

Identifying our myths is an important first step in overcoming them. We each entertain some fantasy regarding the way we would like things to ideally unfold. Our task is to recognize the times when that fantasy becomes so strong that we refuse to accept what is.

The alternative to mythical thinking is *living in truth.* John 8:32 records Jesus' familiar words: "You shall know the truth, and the truth shall make you free." At another time He actually identified Himself as the very embodiment of truth: "Everyone who is of the truth hears My voice" (John 18:37).

OVERCOMING MYTHICAL THINKING

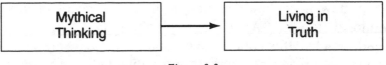

Figure 8-2

Truth can be defined as that which proceeds from the mouth of God. Whereas human philosophies conjure up ideas and concepts that purport to relay the truth, we can be assured that the Word of God is reliable, and thereby truthworthy, as we lay foundations for knowing how to handle our circumstances.

What does God say about the human experience? His message is mixed. There is some good news, some bad news. Life is neither all wonderful, nor all miserable. To break the hold of mythical thinking we can choose to forge a pattern of living anchored in all aspects of God's truth, rather than in just the parts that sound appealing.

First, there is ugly truth. It is an irrefutable fact that we will contend with many forms of pain as long as we live on this side of heaven. There is no such thing as a person perfectly balanced in emotional stability. No perfect marriage exists. All children will disappoint. Friends will not always be capable or willing to be fully tuned in. Churches will let some people fall through the cracks. Trusted leaders will make poor choices. Good people will experience major setbacks. Seem depressing? It is! And yet positive transformation cannot occur until we come to terms with the negative side of life.

A woman spoke with me at a seminar after I had outlined how our sinfulness causes sure emotional difficulty. "I hope you're not going to give us any more negative information," she chided. "After all, if you've lived in stress the only thing you need is positive thoughts." Though I appreciated her desire for something to hope in, I knew she would find increased stress if she tried to shut out all references to pain.

When I counseled with Angie, the anxiety-laden young woman with the "perfect" background, we discussed the paradox of how acceptance of ugly truth could result in greater emotional stability. "When you think about it," I told her, "you already practice this concept in certain ways. For example, suppose you are planning an afternoon outing with your children, but it gets spoiled because of a rain storm. You don't like having your plans ruined, but you just make alternative plans. It's not the end of your day."

"Well that's easy to do because everyone knows it's going to rain sometimes," she replied.

"That's precisely my point. In the same way, let's allow for those times when you are going to feel low or when your husband is insensitive or your children are uncooperative. As sure as rain, those things will happen." When we accept the inevitability of imperfection, we respond to our problems with less self-centeredness and more humility.

Living in truth is most difficult, though, when events or memories are extremely bad. For instance, I have spoken to innumerable people, mostly women, who recall a childhood with horrific experiences of sexual abuse or neglect or rejection. They ask why. "Why did I have to suffer so innocently at the hand of someone so imbalanced?"

There are answers, theological and psychological, to this question. But frankly, they tend not to help much. When a person has suffered to this extreme, no explanation is full enough. The pain keeps us from feeling consoled by high intellect.

In extreme cases of pain, the sufferer needs to determine not to respond in black-or-white thinking. For instance, it does no good to lightly brush off the suffering with the notion "It happens." Nor is it helpful to drape oneself in a victim's identity that allows a blaming, hateful attitude to take root.

Jeremiah 17:9 says bluntly, "The heart is more deceitful than all else and is desperately sick; who can understand it?" Living in truth means that we acknowledge that people can be greatly deranged. Many times they choose to unload their dysfunction on others rather than working it through in a healthy manner. But living in truth also means that each of us can choose not to become so caught in our own responses of pride, fear, loneliness, inferiority, and anger that we are held captive by injustice.

The opposite side of ugly truth is that we can be overcomers. Paul wrote, "If God is for us, who can be against us?" (Romans 8:31 NIV). While He is allowing sin to run its course, He also is enacting His plan to redeem His own from sin. We will contend with pain no more once we are fully glorified in heaven. And as we await that day we can choose to be conformed to His character in a way that will lead to strength and peace, even in the midst of struggle. That was the message Christ offered while mingling among us. He did not remove all pain immediately, but He promised that as we follow Him, He will show us the way through it.

The person who drops mythical thinking will notice a shift in attitudes and responses. For example, the following illustrations show the alternative responses to the situations presented earlier in this chapter:

- A husband is frustrated by his wife's finicky ways. But rather than trying to change her entire disposition, he realizes that he can state his needs without coercion and set boundaries when helpful. Beyond that, he accepts the fact that she may always be more uptight than he is.
- The secretary with the inconsiderate boss decides that it is unproductive to whisper about him behind his back. Instead, she knows it is his choice to be in a foul mood, but she is under no obligation to respond in kind.
- A minister experiences a bout with depression. Though he does not like the problem, he realizes that other men and women of God have been through similar circumstances, but without losing their overall ability to relate His will to others.
- A mother with two misbehaving children in the grocery story still feels tense because of their disobedience. But rather than sinking into utter humiliation, she realizes that virtually every parent knows the frustration of being shown up by little ones. She is not alone.

Personal stability does not come when we are able to find the ideal and dwell there perpetually. It comes when we reconcile ourselves to the dual facts that pain exists, yet God is providing the way to get through the pain.

9

BALANCING YOUR SELF-IMAGE

The book of Ecclesiastes was written by a man trying to make sense of who he was. In his brief discourse, the author (presumed to be Solomon) uses the word *vanity* approximately forty times. The theme echoed throughout the book is "vanity of vanities, all is vanity." Solomon had tried to find himself through education, politics, sex, pleasure, religion. But his pursuits came up futile. He was discovering that there was no human way to make peace with his world. Solomon's problem was that he really did not know himself.

As ancient as Solomon's problem is, it is a problem that still plagues people today. Civilizations have come and gone, knowledge has increased, cultural habits have changed, yet human nature remains the same. Even now in the age of computerized technology and presumed intellectual enlightenment, anxiety-ridden people still ask, "Who am I? What am I to think about the way I should live?" Many live their lives without arriving at a satisfactory conclusion. Not knowing the questions to ask or the directions to turn, they exist without a well-conceived image of themselves. It is no surprise to discover that these are the very people most prone to emotional and relational struggles. When we experience crises with self-identity, we will surely experience crises in the everyday stresses of living.

Our image of self should be clearly delineated if we are to succeed in making peace with our emotions. What we believe about self directly impacts how we interact with the surrounding world. With a self-image that is stable and founded on biblical truths, we can properly operate spiritually, emotionally, and relationally. Conversely, as the self-image is distorted, we become thwarted in those same areas of living.

Self-image can be defined as the sum total of the individual's beliefs, thoughts, and impressions about self. It is a mental filtering system through which the individual interacts with his environment. Self-image is not something we are born with; rather, it is learned. Literally thousands of experiences, particularly those in the formative years, are recorded in a person's subconscious memory bank. Through the years those experiences gradually form the foundation for the guiding thoughts, beliefs, and impressions that determine how we present ourselves to the world.

One or two events do not shape our view of self. Rather, self-image is forged by the repetition of basic patterns of experience. For example, we all have had experiences in which we felt rejected by an authority figure. But many people have had more positive experiences than negative. Therefore, those negative experiences may not necessarily outweigh the positives to the extent that the self-image is permanently damaged. Likewise, each person has a certain amount of resiliency that allows the negative input to be absorbed without completely undermining the self-image.

Conversely, some people who have seemingly healthy backgrounds behave as if they have a weak self-image. Any number of factors can produce a negative self-image. This might include one's inborn personality type, unusual influences on the family life (such as many moves or extended family problems), or hidden negative messages that may not be easy to consciously read.

Cheryl seemingly had a healthy childhood. She was the middle of three children. She made good grades in school and participated in a fair amount of extracurricular activities. Her dad had a good job, her mother stayed at home, and neither was particularly abrasive in family communications. Yet as an adult, Cheryl had repeated problems in maintaining friendships. She had a critical, judgmental spirit that alienated her from her husband and three children, and also caused her to lose several potential friendships. She contended inwardly with anxiety and impatience, and often her emotions became so powerful that she could not reason well with anyone.

Self-image cannot always be discerned by counting the number of positive versus negative statements received in childhood.

In spite of her problems, Cheryl told me that she had a very positive self-image. She was extremely protective of her original family as she described them in nearly flawless terms. But through counseling she learned that many of the seemingly positive messages she had received from her family had underlying messages that caused her to subconsciously doubt herself.

For instance, Cheryl had been taught to think highly of herself—but at the expense of others. She was OK because she could outperform her peers. As a result, her self-image was anchored in a false pride that caused her to fear others who might have ideas or perceptions equal to or better than hers. Also, she learned to cling so unwaveringly to her convictions that she reacted insecurely if someone challenged her beliefs. She had been instructed to be careful in performing tasks, but the teaching was so strong that she developed fear and paranoia if anyone reacted negatively to her performances. What is more, she had a strong take-charge temperament that caused her to view her world in black-and-white terms. This decreased her ability to be flexible with people and circumstances that did not fit her mold.

Cheryl's example illustrates that self-image cannot always be discerned by counting the number of positive versus negative statements received in childhood. Our minds absorb the many subtleties in our interactions with significant others even when we are unaware of it. Her example illustrates that we can best interpret how we received early input by analyzing such factors as outer behavior, emotional manifestations, relationship attitudes, and spiritual maturity.

As one who believes in the depravity of mankind, I assume that every human is susceptible to weaknesses in self-image. That is so for two reasons: (1) we are imperfect in our abilities to integrate godly thoughts about who we are; (2) we are exposed daily to an imperfect world that either intentionally or unintentionally sends messages inconsistent with God's ideals.

With that in mind, let's examine self-image in a twofold manner. First, we'll explore some of Scripture's direct teachings about who we are. Second, we'll examine some of the ways our emotions indicate that our self-image is inconsistent with those biblical truths.

WHAT WE ARE

A man once complained to me that he was in a state of confusion as he tried to understand the Bible. He did not know how to mesh seemingly inconsistent messages, such as our inability to flee from sin with the instruction to be perfect as God Himself is perfect. At times God's Word seems to elevate humanity, at other times it offers harsh rebuke. Because the Bible is wholly true, our task is to integrate its teachings into a unified balance.

At least four truths can be gleaned from Scripture to guide us in knowing what to believe about ourselves: (1) we are created; (2) we are special; (3) we are inept; and (4) we can be strengthened. A balanced self-image takes each of these truths into full account.

WE ARE CREATED

The fact that we are created beings seems obvious to those who learned the creation story from childhood. Logic would indicate that all matter had a beginning and someone who put it into being. Genesis 2:7 states clearly that God formed humanity from the dust of the ground and breathed life into his nostrils. Trying to conceive how God made something out of nothing is so astounding that it is impossible to fully grasp creation's process. Yet it had to start somewhere with someone. It is sheer folly to assume that something arose haphazardly without the word of the Creator.

As logical as it may seem to believe that there had to be an original decree from God to put matter into being, the majority of scientists choose to suspend that logic in favor of the absurdity of the theory of evolution. Because their viewpoint has so powerfully contradicted longstanding Christian beliefs about creation, it is important that we understand the philosophical implications of each view. This will directly impact what we will ultimately believe about the self.

Suppose for a moment that you were not created by God but, instead, you evolved in a mysterious way from the lowest forms of life over billions of years. First, an amoeba appeared on earth, though no one knows exactly how it became a lifeform. (But never mind such trivial details.) The amoeba eventually evolved into a fishy form. Then that fish one day wandered onto land. It eventually developed hair, sprouted legs, and turned into a four-legged creature. And after millions of years it became an ape, then eventually it evolved into a human. No Creator was involved. We just happened.

The concept of evolution, if believed, has enormous implications on our view of self. This theory allows us to assume that we have no allegiance to anyone higher than ourselves. Mankind is the pinnacle of all matter. God is relegated to a mythical status. We have no need to seek counsel from Him or to develop commitments to Him, since He either does not exist or is a passive nonparticipant in life's process.

Furthermore, evolution gives individuals a different feeling of purpose. If we owe no allegiance to the Creator, we are free to go our own way with no concern regarding God's laws. Our purpose in life would be to deify self and seek all that can be gained for self's pleasure. We would assume self-sufficiency in all areas of reasoning, finding meaning only in what self desires.

But if we believe that humanity, in fact, did not evolve but was deliberately given life by almighty God, our beliefs about self are altogether different. First, we would acknowledge that our lives are owed to God. He chose to give us life, so our very existence depends on His will.

Because we are imprinted with
God's image, we are required to
do nothing to prove our worth.

Moreover, as we understand our created status, we find our sense of purpose by knowing Him and willingly conforming to His will. Our purpose in life is not self-centered but God-centered. Each day's activities have significance beyond the moment and can be viewed in the context of eternity. Accepting our created status places devotion to God at the heart of all thoughts and behaviors.

WE ARE SPECIAL

Not only were we created, but Genesis 1:27 states that we were created in the image of God. This, too, has implications for our view of self. Being in God's image, we each have an eternal soul. We have a high form of reasoning. We possess emotions and the ability to relate. We have a spiritual dimension that supersedes the physical. We were made to love and to be loved. We are the only form of creation that can communicate with God.

By acknowledging the image of God within ourselves, we can surmise that each person possesses dignity and honor. Each human has innate worth and value. Because we are imprinted with God's image, we are required to do nothing to prove our worth. We possess it because we exist.

As a boy I was acquainted with many colorful characters due to my father's work. He had a background in prison and institutional chaplaincy, and part of his career consisted of consultations with other chaplains in prisons, retardation facilities, reformatories, and the like. He would take either all or part of the family with him on some of his out-of-town consultations, so I had the experience of seeing first-hand what many people only hear about.

One particular experience comes to mind that illustrated to me the innate value of all individuals. I was about thirteen years old, accompanying my father in a large state facility for the mentally retarded. As was typically the case, the chaplain took us on a tour of the grounds. Our first stop was the women's dormitory, where we stepped into a large open room. There a young woman resident eyed me with great interest, and she came toward me engaged in excited conversation. She was thrilled to meet me, but I honestly didn't know what to do. The woman weighed in excess of two hundred pounds, had a bowl haircut, and an IQ of about 60.

She asked if we could hold hands so she could give me a real tour of the place, and as I looked toward my dad for relief, he had a smile on his face and a twinkle in his eye that said, "Go for it, son. You're about to have the time of your life." So she held my hand and showed me everything important to her—the educational room, the laundry room, the kitchen, the playground. As she entertained me that day she introduced me as her boyfriend to anyone who would stop to listen. (And she knew everyone.) Although I was a self-conscious and insecure teenager, I eventually loosened up and played along. I reasoned to myself that none of my buddies had to know about this, so why not make the most of it.

Later that evening as my dad and I reflected on the day, I heard one of those sermons that kids need. (Being a dad now myself, I reserve the right to preach those same sermons when the moment seems right.) "It's easy to love people who look and act right on the outside. But what you did today was different. You showed love today to someone who could not earn your respect through any great deeds. You were kind to her simply because you chose to be. Right now, that woman feels very special because you openly recognized her worth. And do you know something? That's the way God loves us. Even though we do a poor job of proving ourselves as lovable, He cares for us simply because He sees the value in us that cannot be earned. We are loved because He chooses to consider us worthy. You have learned a valuable lesson today that I hope never leaves you." It hasn't.

Knowing our value to God, our self-image can be powerfully impacted. Primarily, it reminds us that our security is not derived from a human system of approval. Knowing that God has implanted His image in us, we can acknowledge that when humans reject us worth does not diminish. Humans are not the givers of worth. Only God is, and He does not operate on a merit system. He loves us in spite of ourselves because it is His nature to do so.

WE ARE INEPT

It would be wonderful to bask in the knowledge that we are created with purpose and designated by God as special. But there is more to who we are that prohibits us from feeling too smug.

---

*When we choose not to
acknowledge our ineptness,
we ultimately damage our self-image.*

We have already seen that mankind's fall into sin carried emotional repercussions. As a result, there are behavioral, relational, and communication problems we cannot avoid. As hard as we may try, we cannot escape our natural predisposition toward sin. In free will we choose to turn our backs on the life of perfection offered by God. First John 1:8 says, "If we say that we have no sin, we are deceiving ourselves, and the truth is not in us."

When we admit to being sinners, we state that we cannot not sin. A day cannot go by without an error in thought or judgments. We can act insensitively while never intending to do so. We give into emotions such as impatience or anxiety daily. The apostle Paul summarized this in Romans 7:18–19: "For I know that nothing good dwells in me, that is, in my flesh; for the wishing is present in me, but the doing of the good is not. For the good that I wish, I do not do; but I practice the very evil that I do not wish." Paul's anguish over his sinful inclination represents the frustration of every individual who intends to do good but fails.

When we choose not to acknowledge our ineptness, we ultimately damage our self-image. Our beliefs about self would be anchored in lies or misrepresentations of truth. It may seem strange to say that positive transformation begins when we admit our ineptness—in the age of positive thinking that seems out of place. But, in reality, admitting weaknesses can be a profitable step toward change. Once we acknowledge our sinfulness, we have a more focused point of attack. We develop a deeper awareness of our real selves and can use it to motivate us to seek help from the ultimate Counselor.

Richard was despondent. His words had a ring of defeat. He explained to me that he was losing confidence in himself because he failed in a major career challenge. That was the first time he had ever experienced such failure. Previously he had been known in his profession as a great success. His competitors would point to him and say, "I wish I had his capabilities." He made friends easily and enjoyed power and influence.

Because of his failure, Richard lost touch with many former acquaintances. He assumed that they questioned his aptitude and integrity. He felt insecure. And, worse, he was uncertain about how to recapture his past status.

My response caught him off guard. "This could be the best thing that ever happened to you." Certainly I intended no insensitivity, but I knew that Richard had anchored his feelings of worth in his own performances. He had meaning and purpose and value only because he could out-achieve others. I wanted Richard to understand that he could still find contentment in spite of his flaws. He was learning that he was inept, at least in some respects. I hoped he could use this awareness to propel him to a more realistic understanding of how he was equally grounded with other people in his life.

When we admit that we have an ineptness due to our propensity toward imperfection, we lay the groundwork for a belief system that bases self-esteem on a power beyond us.

WE CAN BE STRENGTHENED

The final component of an individual's self-image is the presence of God in his life. But not all people choose to make God part of their lives. As a result, they are incapable of tapping into the strength He offers, which will ultimately reinforce the ineptness that plagues us all. But to those who choose to invite Christ into their lives, strength is readily available.

On the eve of His arrest and crucifixion, Jesus Christ had a long heart-to-heart talk with His disciples. Knowing the finality of the events before Him, Jesus chose His words carefully, emphasizing the most important notions about who He was and what He would do for them. Jesus told the men, "I am the vine, you are the branches; he who abides in Me, and I in Him, he bears much fruit; for apart from Me you can do nothing" (John 15:5).

Jesus underscored our human frailty ("apart from Me you can do nothing"), but He also taught that we can overcome this frailty when we graft our lives into His. As we submit our minds, our behavior, our communications to Him we can find the words of Philippians 4:13 to be true: "I can do all things through [Christ] who strengthens me."

A simple illustration bears this principle out. I can be a patient man, but only to a certain point. As my morning at home begins, small incidents can stand in my way, but I'll handle them. When I begin the day at the office, unexpected phone calls can throw me off schedule, or something may require me to alter my plans. No big deal. Then that meeting with the editor may get postponed, or my lunch time may get cut short. In due time impatience sets in. By the afternoon I'm inwardly agitated when one more thing goes wrong. At home that night I speak curtly when no one seems to care about my issues. Why? I'm a limited man. I can plan to be patient, but my world just won't cooperate. Does this mean that I must remain stuck in a foul mood? No. But to get back on track I'll need God's strength. I'll need to get focused on His desire for me at that moment. That will require time before Him, seeking His favor, committing to let Him fill me with His character when I don't have what it takes.

Can you relate? Each of us is painfully aware of how easy it is to let the sin nature grab the controls in our simplest tasks. The person who becomes strengthened by the power of God deliberately chooses to separate his mind from the sinful enticements that reside within. He can choose instead to respond to the immediate presence of Christ in his life. As that effort is made daily, even hourly, it becomes a pattern, more and more a natural part of the true self.

WHAT WE THINK WE ARE

Because the self-image is learned, it varies greatly from person to person. We find three general patterns of self-image: negatively skewed, positively skewed, and balanced.

NEGATIVELY SKEWED SELF-IMAGE

The majority of people who seek counseling view their self-image negatively. These people usually feel inadequate, especially when handling stress. They commonly indulge in such negative responses as "I can't" and "I don't know." They usually expect negative outcomes to their difficulties.

Frequently, people with negative self-images can recite scriptural promises about God's desire to strengthen us in time of trial. However, when they do recite such Scripture, it is often followed by the word *but*. They may know there is a better way to think, but they do not really believe it is possible to effect the changes that would really help.

For example, a wife may want to feel more positively about herself but says she can't because her husband is not supportive. A single man knows biblical concepts about finding spiritual contentment, but he feels it is impossible because his dating life is unsatisfactory. A church member knows about God's forgiveness but clings to self-doubt because of recent subpar performances. The recurring theme in these illustrations is the acquiescence to negative self-thoughts. Why does this occur? It can be due to one of several reasons:

- *Some people have been given consistently critical messages by significant people.* It is common to hear people complain of family histories laced with criticism and invalidation. When a parent repeats negative sentiments toward a child the repercussions are far-reaching. Self-image can take on the shape of messages given by significant others.

- *Some people have been taught to accept low self-esteem as good.* Sometimes well-intended authority figures, wanting to eliminate false pride, will go so far in emphasizing humility that the beauty of one's position in Christ is destroyed. One woman recalled a Sunday school teacher who said, "You don't want to feel too good about yourself because it will lead to sin." Years later this woman still heard those words ringing in her mind when she was in an upbeat mood. *Cool it,* she would think. *This will surely lead to sin.* She had overlearned this teaching.

- *Some people are taught that positive esteem arises from good performances.* Too often self-image is closely tied to performance. From early childhood we learn to think accepting thoughts when we perform well and rejecting thoughts when we perform poorly. Our standing before humans, rather than our standing before God, becomes the foundation for self-image.

- *Some people are genuinely confused about what others think of them.* Many people have not had much negative input from significant others, but they have not had much positive input either. They assume negative thoughts about themselves only because they have little positive knowledge to build on. When family members keep interactions superficial, a developing child may just assume negative thoughts about himself due to natural tendencies to wonder about personal worth.

POSITIVELY SKEWED SELF-IMAGE

Other individuals have developed an excessively positive view of self. So much focus is placed on the value of self that the recognition of sinfulness is lost. These people either latch exclusively onto teachings of their special value to God or they just declare themselves valuable. When this kind of thinking occurs, self-image becomes dangerously similar to humanistic philosophy.

Quite correctly, people who hold a positive view of self proclaim that our thoughts control our behavior. Then, armed with verses about the value of humanity, they launch into a way of life guided by the "I am the pinnacle of creation" mind-set. Without balance, this thinking can feed false pride. In this skewed mind-set a subtle arrogance can easily occur. People can become so pleased with who they are that they feel little need for repentance.

Persons most prone to a positively skewed mentality are those who rationalize the wrongs in their lives with a carefree shrug.

Robert came to my office at the insistence of his wife after she learned he had been engaged in a long-term affair. During the course of our first visit, he admitted to feelings of anger toward his wife. He acknowledged their communication to be poor, due in large part to his own disinterest. He admitted feeling guilty for having lived a double life for at least a year. But when I suggested that this adultery implied that he must be struggling with self-esteem issues, he balked.

Robert explained to me that he had always been a confident man who felt positively about himself. "Self-image is something I've never had a problem with. I'm my own person, and I like the way I manage most things." He then began exonerating himself of the affair by saying he deserved more than his marriage could offer. He explained that his wife seemed too consumed with chores and their three school-age children, so some positive attention was due him, if not from her then from someone else. He told me that he was a Christian and that God did not want him to be lonely. Ultimately, Robert showed no particular sign of remorse, stating that he only wished he had not been caught.

Persons most prone to a positively skewed mentality are those who rationalize the wrongs in their lives with a carefree shrug. Thinking themselves special, they put on mental blinders when faced with the need to reconcile self to sin. Their mistake is to selectively focus on the ego-inflating truths about self while ignoring or downplaying the humbling truths.

BALANCED SELF-IMAGE

A healthy self-image strikes a realistic balance between our specialness to God and our propensity toward sin. The balanced self-image is optimistic since there is a recognition that God chooses to offer unmerited favor to all who call upon Him. Yet, there is also genuine humility because of the awareness that we can create grief in God due to misdeeds. The positive feeling that results from experiencing God's favor creates unbounded joy for living, whereas the awareness of sin's ugliness prevents arrogance.

The apostle Paul is a model of the balanced view of self. On the one hand, he freely acknowledged that his relationship with Christ created contentment (Philippians 4:11). On the other hand, he spoke quite humbly, referring to himself as the foremost of sinners (1 Timothy 1:15). Many times he spoke of the glorious feeling he had about life, but in each case he gave credit to God rather than to himself.

It was this balance, then, that led to the development of Paul's bond-servant attitude in relation to Christ. As a bond-servant, he realized that he was free to act in whatever way he desired, yet he willfully chose submission to his Lord. He recognized that the grace and mercy of God freed him from all that was negative about sin, and he committed himself to a lifetime of voluntary servitude to Christ. He accepted his special status before God, and he showed his gratitude by offering God his total will. Although most of us will not attain the consistent submission of Paul, we can each choose to live in glad subservience to God.

The person who recognizes both the sinful ways of self and the love that indwells us from God can live in a way that is both humble and confident. Optimistic thoughts about self will not prevent an awareness that we are fortunate to be used of God.

HOW WE PORTRAY OURSELVES

An old adage can reveal our true perspective on our self-image: Actions speak louder than words. Many individuals are not honest with themselves concerning self-image. I have heard many people make bold proclamations about a balanced or a confident self-image when in fact their behavior does not back up the claim. I have concluded that a person's own opinion is not the most reliable way to determine the nature of his self-image. It is more accurate to examine his attitudes, behavior, and emotions.

Notice how self-image is revealed in the five basic areas of emotional struggle and in the psychological barriers to personal growth.

Pride vs. Humility. When self-image is out of balance, either in the positive or negative direction, pride results. A preoccupation with self occurs when we think too highly or too lowly about ourselves. But when we have balance in our self-image, we can know humility—a modest sense of importance accompanied by a realization of personal limits.

Fear vs. Trust In God. When self-image is skewed either to the positive or negative side, fear becomes more prominent. The overly positive person becomes defensive, covering up any personal trait that might make him look human, while the overly negative person flinches easily at the prospect of reminders of rejection. The balanced self-image acknowledges that not all will be well in our world, yet God's guidance will see us through those imperfections.

Loneliness vs. Fellowship. If you are like me, you find it difficult to truly fellowship with a person whose self-image is skewed. The positively skewed person is not able to relate to real life, and the negatively skewed person is too fragile to handle reality. Only when a person carries a balanced awareness of the good and bad qualities of self can there be a genuine linking of spirits.

Inferiority vs. God-given Value. Keep in mind that inferiority not only shows itself in a negatively skewed self-image, but sometimes it masks itself with attempts to appear superior. An out of balance self-image, therefore, reflects one or the other of these manifestations of inferiority. A balanced self-image recognizes that personal worth is stable due to the declarations of God.

Anger vs. Kindheartedness. When people have either a positively or negatively skewed self-image, anger is more likely. The positively skewed person can be irritated when others do not share the same high view of themselves as they think they should. The negatively skewed person easily nurses depression or bitterness. When balance is found in the self-image, anger can be expressed constructively, then it gives way to the commitment to kindness and forgiveness.

Deficient Love vs. Spiritual Well-Being. An imbalanced self-image implies that a person has not reconciled himself to deficient love experiences. The one who clings to a positively skewed view of self is compensating for the lack of real love, and the one who views self too negatively has allowed rejecting people to have too strong a say in personal identity. A balanced self-image indicates that a person has rightfully realized that love will not always be forthcoming from people, while God's love is indeed reliable.

People with an imbalanced self-image are in bondage.

Trained Incompetence vs. Contemplative Thinking. When people have not received the training to sift through their emotional and relational issues, the result is an imbalanced self-image. A positively skewed self-image is invariably accompanied by a "Pollyanna" approach toward life, where real difficulties are just brushed aside. A negatively skewed self-image represents a personal collapse under the assumption that a person can't manage problems. A balanced self-image is anchored in the notion that, whereas not all problems can be solved immediately, with patience they can be overcome in some fashion.

Evaluative vs. Descriptive Emphasis. The out-of-balance self-image represents an overemphasis on the judgments given by others. A person who projects himself too positively is trying to win the game of evaluations, while the person who harbors a negative view of self has conceded defeat in this area. The balanced self-image shows that a person has rightly sidestepped unnecessary human judgments and has accepted instead the proclamation that God shows no condemnation toward His own.

Imperative vs. Free Thinking. People with an imbalanced self-image are in bondage. The positively skewed person feels the need to live up to an ideal agenda of have-tos and shoulds, whereas the negatively skewed person feels he never will be able to meet such expectations. The balanced person experiences freedom. There is a desire to live according to standards and norms, yet it is not applied in such a demanding way that it creates tension and distress.

Mythical vs. Truthful Thinking. Neither the positively nor the negatively skewed self-image is anchored in truth. The overly positive person has assumed that he can, in fact, live up to mythical norms, whereas the overly negative person spends too much time waiting for a utopia that will never occur. The balanced person accepts the fact of personal inadequacy and God's acceptance.

The following chart illustrates that our self-image undergirds all our emotional and psychological issues:

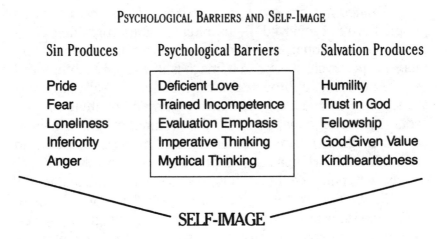

PSYCHOLOGICAL BARRIERS AND SELF-IMAGE

Sin Produces	Psychological Barriers	Salvation Produces
Pride	Deficient Love	Humility
Fear	Trained Incompetence	Trust in God
Loneliness	Evaluation Emphasis	Fellowship
Inferiority	Imperative Thinking	God-Given Value
Anger	Mythical Thinking	Kindheartedness

SELF-IMAGE

Figure 9-1

10

PERSONALITY DISORDERS AND THEIR DISTINCT NEEDS

Two things can be said with certainty: All people are alike; each individual is unique. Does that make any sense?

Romans 5:12 says, "Through one man [Adam] sin entered into the world, and death through sin, and so death spread to all men, because all sinned." We have already discussed that each of us by virtue of our fallen status is "in Adam." As a result, we are all similar in that we struggle with the emotions produced by sin: pride, fear, loneliness, inferiority, anger.

But Scripture also tells us in 1 Corinthians 12:14 that the body is not one member but many. No one is exactly like anyone else. Paul gave the analogy of a human body, saying that one person may function as a "hand," another as an "eye," and another as an "ear." God gives each person a unique blend of spiritual gifts, strengths and weaknesses, preferences, and mannerisms. Personality traits are so numerous that no one personality will ever be exactly duplicated.

All people have the same Adamic nature, but each individual has a unique blend of traits and mannerisms that separates him from the crowd. Although we each need to reconcile ourselves to God through Christ, we all have a different pattern of living out our emotions. These patterns can be identified and understood, thereby making our growth efforts more focused.

These two thoughts, all people are alike and each individual is unique, have strong implications for those seeking to understand themselves better. That is, although the struggles outlined in the previous chapters are pertinent to every individual, some personalities will find certain of those issues standing out more prominently than others. (For instance, one person can relate more to the problems of inferiority or deficient love experiences, whereas another person identifies more keenly with imperative thinking and anger.)

---

*The obsessive-compulsive personality
is distinguished by repetitive,
almost unstoppable, thought patterns.*

In the pages to follow we will examine some of the more common personality disorders studied in psychological circles, with the hope that you will learn to identify your tendencies toward dysfunction, making the necessary corrections. No one will fit singularly into just one of the personality types mentioned. You will discover that you have some of this, a little of that, and a lot of the other. The purpose is to help you identify the "hot spots" that might require greater focus as you seek personal growth.

OBSESSIVE-COMPULSIVE PERSONALITY

The obsessive-compulsive personality is distinguished by repetitive, almost unstoppable, thought patterns that lead to a powerful need to perform according to a rigid system of duties or obligations. Individuals of this personality type tend to be methodical to the extent of inflexibility. They are uncomfortable with change and variations in routine.

Once obsessive-compulsives get a particular idea in mind, they usually cannot let it go until they have made every effort to act upon it. This creates both a fretting spirit and a finicky nature. These people can become particularly frustrated when they have ideas on which they are unable to act. (For example, an obsessive-compulsive may be unable to relax at home knowing there are assignments left hanging at work.) Obsessive-compulsives can be perfectionists who tend to think rigidly. Because of the need to perform "correctly," these individuals are usually uncomfortable with emotions because emotions may interfere with performance. These individuals have an unusual need to appear strong, decisive, and "together," which causes them to experience turmoil in the subjective areas of life—feelings, moments of tenderness, being reflective, and so on.

On the positive side, obsessive-compulsives can be well organized; they can lend logic to problem solving. They can bring order to disarray. Most households would function poorly if we had no sense of structure, so these people are not without merit.

The two most prominent emotional struggles of an obsessive-compulsive are anger and guilt (a spinoff of hidden feelings of inferiority). Anger is frequently displayed by means of habitually critical thoughts. These individuals usually have high levels of frustration with family members, schedules, and the lack of orderliness. They tend to have such a hard-driven need to perform correctly that they become distraught when people and circumstances do not suit their desires. They need to explore the various ways they express anger and, more important, the underlying reasons for excessive amounts of that emotion. Not all the anger will be found as wrong, but moderation will be needed.

Beneath the anger, fueling the intensity of frustration, is usually a powerful struggle with guilt. Depending on whether the obsessive-compulsive is openly domineering or driven to please others, the guilt can be either subtle or obvious. In the case of the openly domineering obsessive-compulsive, the guilt tends to be obscure. The individual may not openly admit feeling guilty and may in fact present an aura of superiority. But it is hidden inferiority that propels the drive to achieve. In the case of a more subservient obsessive-compulsive, however, guilt is more readily admitted. This person is usually more open-minded and quicker to reexamine his need to perform for worth that is already God-given.

The psychological barrier most prominent in the obsessive-compulsive is imperative thinking. This personality type is driven by "supposed tos," "have tos," and "had betters." Usually this person can point to a long-standing habit, beginning in childhood, of needing to comply with an endless list of rules and regulations. Because the individual may not have felt permission to be free and relaxed, the drive to be a performer was heightened. The obsessive-compulsive should concentrate on reducing imperative thinking and accepting responsible freedom.

HISTRIONIC PERSONALITY

Unlike the obsessive-compulsive personality, which is unnaturally driven by logic and the need to perform precisely, the histrionic personality is governed by emotional highs and lows. The subjective dominates this personality. These individuals tend to be more dramatic and excitable, particularly when variations in routine occur. When expressing their feelings (which they do frequently) it is common for these individuals to exaggerate and use superlatives. They tend to have a powerful need for affirmation and attention, which at times produces reactionary behavior (responding before thinking). They are very people-oriented.

Because of their active, emotional nature, histrionic individuals often have charming, gregarious personalities. They have a natural ability to speak about personal matters, and they tend to put most people at ease, particularly in social settings. But this same gregarious, social characteristic is often instrumental in bringing out immature personality traits. Because they need to relate on an emotional, personal level, these persons tend to be easily upset when the desired level of attention is not received. They may have hidden fears that the "white knight" who will offer them the relational stability and emotional stimulation they desire will never appear.

Perhaps the most prominent emotional struggle for the histrionic personality is loneliness. They may have surface problems with such issues as anger, depression, or worry. But under the surface they have the feeling of being misunderstood and isolated. These individuals, because of an intense desire to be emotionally connected with others, tend to feel that their relationships with family members and friends fall short of their hopes. Consequently, loneliness is germinated and grows into thought patterns that produce anger, depression, and worry.

A second major emotional struggle for the histrionic personality is fear. Typically, the fear of being rejected and abandoned is commonly present (consciously or subconsciously) in these individuals. They are often in a state of apprehension and doubt even when they appear to be happy and full of life. They have an ever-present dread of being disliked or shunned. This can cause them to be guarded in exposing their full slate of weaknesses, or perhaps they may appear ultrasensitive if someone expresses disagreement or rejection.

The psychological barrier most common to the histrionic personality is deficient love. The individual may have a background in which love and acceptance were hard to come by. In many cases, one or both parents lacked the ability to express warmth, leaving that person with a need to look elsewhere for "strokes." Not feeling fulfilled in the area of love, a dependency on others was born.

Narcissists approach relationships with a "what's in it for me" mind-set.

A second possible scenario involves a family background in which love was given in large doses, to the extent that they were not encouraged to develop emotional independence based on a close walk with God. This implies mythical thinking. In this case, they may enter adult life seeking mates and sets of friends who will fill the enormous shoes of the original families. They will most likely meet heartache instead, because mates do not exist who can meet the needs of histrionics in the impossible manner they have come to expect.

NARCISSISTIC PERSONALITY

Ancient Greek literature tells the mythical story of a young man named Narcissus, who leaned over the edge of a pond to refresh himself and, upon seeing his own reflection in the water, fell in love with himself. From that story, we derive the term *narcissism*. The narcissistic personality has an excessive, inappropriate admiration for himself to the extent of self-absorption. Narcissists have a difficult time relating to the personal needs of others because of an incessant desire to focus on self. In conversation they have a tendency to repetitively draw the subject of conversation to themselves. For example, when someone is telling a narcissistic person about a personal experience, the narcissist will predictably say, "Oh, that reminds me of a time when I . . ."

This personality type tends to have a long pattern of broken relationships. Although acquaintances may first find them charming and adventuresome, they will eventually discover that these individuals find it impossible to show love and concern. In time, their tendency to be manipulative emerges along with a push for special privileges and considerations. Their level of communication is typically shallow, and their ability to relate to others' feelings proves to be next to nothing.

Narcissists approach relationships with a "what's in it for me" mind-set. When their needs are not met, they are ready to jump ship. They have a low tolerance for differentness but a high need for others to maintain special interest in them.

The prominent emotional struggle in the narcissistic personality is sinful pride. There is an exaggerated feeling of self-importance and a tremendous preoccupation with self's desires and preferences. These individuals have succumbed to Satan's temptation to place self in a godlike position. A positively skewed self-image prompts them to promote their self-worth and ignore their sinfulness and character defects. They need to concentrate on understanding and appropriating biblical selflessness.

Mythical thinking is the psychological barrier most common to narcissists. The delusion of self-importance leads to other delusions. They assume that other people should come to their senses and recognize how wonderful they are. They unrealistically imagine that life would be perfect if only the right person (who worshipfully adored them) could be found. These individuals come from a family background of excessive praise or of the other extreme in which little love was offered, thereby creating a compensatory need for love.

BORDERLINE PERSONALITY

The borderline personality is characterized by unpredictable moodiness and inappropriate emotional displays. The term *borderline* stems from the fact that on first impression these individuals seem normal, but on further examination something in their personalities seems incomplete. They seem to teeter on the brink of breakdown. When life presents no problems, they are just like everyone else, but when difficulties erupt, look out!

They differ from the histrionic personality—which is also highly emotional—in that their impulsive behavior and self-destructive actions may include alcohol abuse, sexual promiscuity, binge eating (as in the case of bulimia), and wasteful spending habits. These individuals dread being alone. They feel they must be involved in activities with others and will often compromise their well-taught principles to become connected with others. They need a high level of stimulation and are quickly bored and easily led astray.

In addition to volatile emotional and behavioral patterns, borderline personalities have a high level of uncertainty regarding self-identity. You might say they suffer from a disintegrated self-image. They may have problems feeling satisfied with work or in marriage because they do not know themselves well enough to know what they want. They may make a commitment to one person, lifestyle, or hobby and in a matter of months prefer something else. They may not even know what that something else is, but they know they want something else. The result may be extreme anger and depression, even suicidal depression.

Although these individuals may need to focus initially on the emotional issues of anger and depression, they will need to eventually concentrate on restructuring the self-image. Typically they come from a family background that emphasized superficial qualities, such as charming social skills or athletic prowess—or worse, a background in which love was absent. The result is a foundation of insecurity, which in adult life brings problems with self-identity. That explains the propensity toward promiscuity, craving money, and similar characteristics. They need to learn that people and things and activities do not give meaning to life as much as spiritual well-being does.

In a silent way, passive-aggressive
individuals can be controlling.

Borderline personalities often have a background of trained incompetence. Their learning has centered on irrelevant matters, and they have little understanding of such important matters as handling emotions, maintaining personal relationships, and loving without succumbing to sexual arousal. As long as they lack insight into their psychological make-up, they will continue to succumb to their prideful impulses. Though it is not natural to them yet, borderline personalities need to learn not to panic when alone or rejected, determining instead to draw upon inner confidence that they can face life's problems.

PASSIVE-AGGRESSIVE PERSONALITY

The passive-aggressive personality is typified by inner frustrations and anxieties that are kept hidden and therefore unresolved. These individuals have an ongoing problem of unresolved anger (which they refer to as frustration or hurt), and this causes them a host of problems in interpersonal relationships. They tend to procrastinate, be chronically late for appointments, and be forgetful and lazy. They are often indecisive, not because they have no ability to make sound decisions, but because they would prefer to let someone else take the heat if problems occur. They may seek advice from friends and then ignore it.

In a silent way, passive-aggressive individuals can be controlling. They tend to have a stubborn streak, a critical nature, and a desire to do things according to their own preferences behind the backs of others. In that sense, they may have sneaky ways of being manipulative. It is often difficult to get true commitments from these individuals, and the commitments that are given may prove half-hearted. Hesitant to assume leadership roles, they are often attracted to strong authority figures. Yet eventually their stubbornness creates an unwillingness to be dominated, which sets painful power struggles into motion. They may struggle with marital or family problems, but, when confronted with their need to take responsibility in finding solutions, they tend to point the finger of blame elsewhere.

The passive-aggressive's most prominent emotional struggle is anger, but the anger is influenced by deep fears. Inwardly, passive-aggressive individuals desire control (sinful pride), but they are afraid that if they are blatant in their maneuvering for control they will be squelched. This fear creates a strong habit of defensiveness and outward phoniness, which over time leads to emptiness in relations. This emptiness eventually turns into anger, but, because of the fear of openness, the anger is held in and is expressed in passive ways. Frequently these individuals become candidates for major depression. Their steps to personal transformation begin with determining how their hidden anger is expressed in an abrasive manner. They need to learn to be more assertive without expressing aggressiveness. In addition, they need to replace fearful defensiveness with trust in God.

In most cases, the prominent psychological barrier to emotional stability for passive-aggressives is imperative thinking. Because of their secret desire for control, they impose a long inner list of shoulds and ought tos on family and friends. If they can replace imperative thinking with freedom and learn to accept themselves and others as they are, they will diminish interpersonal stress.

DEPRESSIVE PERSONALITY

People who have long-standing struggles with depression tend to have either passive-aggressive or depressive personalities. The depressive personality differs from the passive-aggressive in that the tendency toward manipulation and defensiveness is not blatant, nor is there the tendency to get caught in power struggles. Depressive persons have virtually quit on life.

Depressive personalities are distinguished by having long-standing feelings of futility with their own abilities to handle the day-to-day tensions of work or family environments. Feelings of rejection or of just not fitting in play a prominent role in their mental outlook. These individuals suffer from feelings of hopelessness and are often unable to enjoy normally pleasant events. They have lapses of time in which their memory does not serve them well, and there are times when their concentration levels are low. They may think in self-flagellating terms, become easily worried, and feel that life is meaningless. Their motivation to reach out to family and friends is poor. They may have a lowered sex drive and consequently a history of failure or unhappiness in marital relationships. They may frequently suffer from suicidal thoughts and a desire to die.

Besides the repression of anger, the depressive personality also struggles with inferiority. These individuals have a sinking feeling of unworthiness and despair. They commonly assume that they do not have the same set of tools that enables them to tackle life as productively as others. In many cases they struggle under false guilt from the notion that they are bad. They think in evaluative, comparative terms, and their self-evaluations are unusually harsh.

Most depressive personalities can recall a background in which they lacked satisfying experiences of love. Their parents were either too critical, too uninvolved, or too protective, not allowing them to fend for themselves in the real world. As a result, a negatively skewed self-image was developed. As these individuals developed in late adolescence and early adulthood, they probably had bland social circumstances, preferring to stay with small groups of people, avoiding new or adventuresome environments. In a large percentage of cases, these individuals marry the first or second person they date. Later in adult life they may question the wisdom of that decision.

A major obstacle for the depressive person is the tendency to feel defeated. This implies trained incompetence. Since these individuals tend to have a history of disappointment, they do not expect their attempts to change or find a lasting cure to succeed. Their feelings of inadequacy lead to the hope (and even expectation) that other people will accomplish any needed changes for them. They secretly long for someone to wave a magic wand, causing their depression to lift. But as long as those around them continue to "rescue" them from responsibility, they will never make the effort to find their own road to peace.

SOCIOPATHIC PERSONALITY

The sociopathic personality is habitually unable to be responsible. These individuals have an impulsive, pleasure-seeking drive that causes them to shun normal moral standards when those standards get in the way of what they want. They frequently experience problems with alcohol abuse, sexual deviancies, or financial difficulties. Although many have higher than average intelligence, they often have a history of poor school or job performances. Living according to hedonistic principles, they seek good times and have a low tolerance for interference of any kind. They are extremely sensitive to any hint of accountability.

As people try to develop intimacy with sociopathic individuals, they become disillusioned by the sociopath's propensity for lying, cheating, and sneaky manipulation.

A simple example of sociopathic behavior is a business-person who pads his expense account by a few dollars or a housewife who lies about what she really did during the day. A more explicit illustration is the con artist who sells deals to un-suspecting buyers, then leaves them with nothing to show for it.

Sociopaths do not always seem to have particular person-ality deficiencies because they are skilled in creating positive first impressions. And as long as relationships maintain a su-perficial nature, their selfishness tends not to surface. However, as people try to develop intimacy with sociopathic individuals, they become disillusioned by the sociopath's propensity for ly-ing, cheating, and sneaky manipulation. Also, as relationships develop, it becomes evident that these individuals have little depth. (They may be able to speak in seemingly deep thoughts, but that is usually phony.) What is worse, when problems in relationships occur, these individuals seem to lack any true sense of guilt, demonstrated by the fact that they are prone to repeating their mistakes. They do not seem to learn from mis-takes (except how to be more careful about not getting caught). They seem to have a knack for getting stuck in the same ruts as before.

Although on first impression they may present a friendly, likable disposition, time proves that people of this personality type have an inability to sustain love. They experience the psy-chological barrier of deficient love. Typically they were either under the care of parents who were extremely strict or extremely loose in discipline. That does not necessarily mean that the parents did not love them but that these individuals did not perceive satisfactory love. Consequently, they learned early in life that the only way to get anywhere in relationships was to exploit.

Anger is the most prominent emotion in these individuals. It is the driving energy behind their rebellious, free-spirited behavior. Although the anger can be rationalized to be a normal need for self-preservation, it tends to have aggressive overtones, since little consideration is given to how it affects others. It is demonstrated more clearly when sociopaths are required to submit to structures or strong authorities. When they feel controlled or even hampered or confronted, a nasty temper emerges. Their anger problems stem from sinful pride and an assumption of immunity from normal standards and guidelines. Only by submitting to an accountable structure will these individuals find personal peace.

DEPENDENT PERSONALITY

The dependent personality does not necessarily have chronic problems with anger or depression or worry (though that may sometimes be the case). These individuals may, in fact, have a pleasant demeanor and a true servant's heart. If anything, they can be too kind and cooperative. These people not only do not mind taking on menial servitude, they actually enjoy it. They are often known as friendly and loyal. Dependent personalities are characterized by the fact that they have an uncanny knack of finding themselves in relationships where they are in subordination to domineering figures. Their willingness to serve and be kind can actually be exaggerated to the point that they are too tolerant of abusive or unfriendly circumstances. Their willingness to let others take responsibility in major areas of decision-making requires the dependent personality to accept a passive posture as a given in life. An example would be a marital partner who subserviently bows to the demanding nature of his mate, even though the demands are extreme and the mate is obviously taking advantage of the partner's good nature.

The background experience of this personality type tends to be one of trained incompetence. That is, a parent may have specifically taught or modeled the idea that it does no good to take a firm stand in any issue of controversy, so it would be just as well to smile and do whatever is necessary to keep peace. In learning such a way of thinking, these individuals are specifically denied the encouragement to struggle with tough options and preferences.

Also, these people tend to place strong emphasis on their evaluative standing before others. They can be very conscientious about their good or bad grades, desiring to have only good marks on their ledger. They do not want to displease anyone.

Subtly underlying the dependent personality are struggles with fear and guilt. These individuals like to maintain order in life, with little friction. That need can be so great that they become easily threatened by friction, prompting them to do whatever is necessary to keep peace, even if it involves accepting abuse. This habit of trying too hard to keep peace can cause them to take responsibility for the actions of others, sometimes leading them to make excuses for other's flaws or to take blame that is not theirs. This feeds a guilt complex, since they begin feeling badly about themselves whenever someone else strays.

Dependent personalities often face problems with troublesome children who have learned to be manipulative and troublesome marriages in which the spouse has subconsciously accepted the invitation to treat the mate with no respect. In addition to realigning the thoughts guiding them into fear and guilt, they need to learn assertiveness and appropriate expressions of anger as outlined in Ephesians 4:15, 26.

CYCLOTHYMIC PERSONALITY

The cyclothymic personality experiences sharp mood swings between elation and depression. You might say that *cy-*

clothymic is the baby brother to *manic-depressive* (bipolar) illness. Either extreme can last from a couple of days to several weeks. And interspersed between the extremes may even be lulls in which normalcy reigns.

When cyclothymic individuals are in the high mood they may appear to be quite enthusiastic, outgoing, pleased with life, and optimistic. They will typically laugh easily and heartily, sometimes even appearing to be giddy. During those times they will attack work with gusto and can be quite productive and creative in thought. There is a danger that in this time of euphoria they may become too impulsive, overextending themselves in emotional commitments, finances, and scheduling.

The cyclothymic typically refuses to acknowledge problems when things are good and is distraught when things are bad.

When the low mood hits, as it predictably does, it comes in part from the knowledge that the high feeling cannot last forever. So the wonderfully happy times come crashing down to disillusionment. During the low moods, cyclothymics can be quite irritable and negative. No amount of encouragement is enough. They question their ability to perform in spite of evidence that speaks well of their abilities. And they view the more effervescent side of their personality as phony. During this low period, they have self-derogatory thoughts accompanied by feelings of loneliness and unhappiness. It is difficult to speak rationally with them at this point, since they are determined to mope and brood.

It is not easy to pinpoint the most specific struggles in this personality type since they can be so varied. In all probability, however, they can be traced to a defensive nature and the inability to accept reality. Their family background may have been based on the mythical idea that enough hard work would create ideal circumstances. There was probably an inability, even a fear, of discussing emotions. If emotions were expressed, they were not understood. As a result, the cyclothymic typically refuses to acknowledge problems when things are good and is distraught when things are bad.

These individuals make self-improvement efforts during a depressive period. At that time they are most open to examining their fears and their mythical thinking. But then they may forget their growth goals as soon as the good mood returns. As they gain insight into their personality, they need to remind themselves to keep up improvement efforts during times when their moods are positive.

SCHIZOID PERSONALITY

The schizoid personality is identified by a chronic inability to develop normal social skills and interpersonal relationships. In fact, these individuals appear to have little ability to express warmth or to engage in the most casual of interactions. They have what is termed "flat affect," or a deficiency in the realm of emotional expression or awareness. When praise is given, they seem unimpressed; when criticism is offered, they appear apathetic. They can be described as plodding through life with dull detachment and passive aloofness. It is no great wonder to discover that they often lack friends or even pleasant acquaintances. If they marry, they tend to be homebodies, but it is not unusual for them to either marry late or not at all.

Usually the schizoid person is motivated toward personal transformation through struggles with depression. However, the depression experienced by schizoid individuals does not always have the same precipitators as the depression experienced by individuals of more normal traits. In most cases of depression the emotion is set up by experiences of rejection, repressed anger, or unusually stressful environmental pressures. But in the case of schizoid individuals, it is usually the by-product of a lifelong history of isolation and frustration due to an inability in knowing how to relate to others.

Lasting improvement may depend on the availability of a support group who will include these people in their plans. Having someone to show an interest in them will be highly therapeutic. They tend not to be insightful, so making peace with themselves tends to be the by-product of success in relationships. In order to contribute to their own growth process, schizoids need to learn ways of showing appreciation to those they interact with. They need to persistently expose themselves to social groups that are naturally accepting and patient with their less than perfect social skills.

Being sensitive to any hint of appearing weak, paranoid individuals find it difficult to admit fear.

The psychological barrier most prominent in these individuals is deficient love. That does not mean they necessarily came from a background without love (although that is sometimes the case). Sometimes, there is a problem in their ability to perceive love or to express their thoughts and feelings. That could possibly be due to biochemical problems, to the parents' inability to communicate openly, or to early trauma that inhibited emotional expression. Schizoid personalities will make the greatest therapeutic strides as they take the risk of being open and letting others love them.

PARANOID PERSONALITY

The paranoid personality is characterized by an extremely sensitive emotional state in which the individual's feelings are easily hurt. These individuals tend to be guarded in their words and actions, often suspecting the worst about others. Their defensive nature is prominent and prompts them to fend off criticism or even mild confrontation with denial, rationalization, and blame. Because of the intensity of this defensiveness, they tend to keep their distance in relationships and have a hard time developing closeness. In some cases they are friendly as long as the conversation stays away from anything personal, but they rarely exchange any warmth.

Quite often, anger is the most prominent emotion in their lives. Their need for distance lends itself to a critical nature, usually accompanied by cynicism and skepticism. But although anger is the most publicly displayed emotion, the real issue to be confronted is deep-seated fear. Being sensitive to any hint of appearing weak, paranoid individuals find it difficult to admit fear. Yet these individuals need to learn to recognize their hypersensitivity as evidence of their fear of being out of control and the fear of rejection. The paranoia is a cover for a weak ego.

Fueling the fear is a stronger than average amount of pride. These individuals tend to be preoccupied with their own importance to the extent that they view themselves as being one of the few normal individuals in an otherwise mixed-up world. This pride causes them to be secretive and controlling, and it pushes them to take positions of leadership so that they can call the shots and not be left to submit to anyone else's authority. If they cannot find leadership in a large group, they will become dominant among a small circle of people, such as family or business associates. It is difficult for these individuals to practice submission to God, since they interpret submission as an invitation to painful vulnerability.

The most prominent psychological barrier for the paranoid person is imperative thinking. Inevitably, these individuals have been reared in backgrounds where life was black-and-white. Suggestions were not offered nor were opinions truly discussed. Rather, rules were to be abided by regardless of varying opinions.

In befriending the paranoid personality, great care must be taken to establish trust from the beginning of the relationship. Because confrontation is so difficult with these individuals, friends and family members must first demonstrate the ability and willingness to listen to their point of view.

Figure 10-1 summarizes the key elements of each personality type.

CONCLUSION

After attending several seminars detailing the various personality types, a man smiled as he told me, "I had no idea that I was so crazy until I heard the speaker identify the traits of these personalities. I saw myself in almost every one of them!" The truth is, if we took the basic traits of our personalities and examined them in an exaggerated fashion, each of us could place a "neurotic" label on ourselves. Since we are all sinners it is no surprise to uncover weaknesses in ourselves.

But the purpose of explaining these personality types is not to force an uncomfortable title upon someone. Rather, the purpose is to identify the key emotional and behavioral traits that block the process of peace. By facing the most formidable issues, we can begin to restructure our thoughts and behaviors.

PERSONALITY DISORDERS

Personality Type	Distinguishing Features	Emotional Problems
Obsessive-Compulsive	Rigid system of duties and obligations; repressed emotions; perfectionistic	Anger; guilt; imperative thinking
Histrionic	Highly emotional; outgoing; reactor; personal; need for acceptance	Loneliness; fear; deficient love experience
Narcissistic	Self-centered; impressed by self; broken relationships; shallow; "user"	Pride; positively skewed self-image; mythical thinking
Borderline	Unpredictable moodiness; emotional; self-destructive; Who am I?	Out of balance self-image; trained incompetence; anger
Passive-Aggressive	Repressed anger; indecisive; controlling; critical; manipulative; stubborn	Fear; pride; imperative thinking
Depressive	Rejected; discouraged; hopeless; poor concentration; lowered libido	Inferiority; guilt; anger; deficient love experiences
Sociopathic	Poor morals; superficial; cheating; repetitive mistakes; friendly	Inability for love; anger; pride
Dependent	Dominated; passive; too subservient; pleasant	Emotional incompetence; fear; guilt; need for assertiveness
Cyclothymic	Sharp mood swings; impulsive; easily discouraged; brooding	Defensiveness; poor reality testing; mythical thinking
Schizoid	Flat affect; detached; unimpressed; dull	Loneliness; deficient love experiences; depression
Paranoid	Hypersensitive; defensive; no warmth; cynical	Fear; pride; hidden weak ego

Figure 10-1

Part 3

Putting Insights
into Practice

11

EXPERIENCING THE PRESENCE OF CHRIST

I have often wondered what it would be like to have a private, face-to-face discussion with Jesus Christ. We would certainly have a lot to talk about. I would be eager to hear Him recount His version of some of the extraordinary experiences of His earthly ministry: the feeding of the five thousand, healing the paralytic man carried to Him by his friends, the encounter with the woman caught in the act of adultery, His trial and crucifixion. I would listen carefully as He would tell about the thoughts and feelings associated with those events. I would try to learn how He determined the course of action to take in each circumstance, and I would try to understand His personality so that I could incorporate His character into my own. Surrounded by the peacefulness of His voice, I would feel content.

I am sure that He would be equally eager to hear *my* thoughts and experiences. He would give me a chance to tell about my burdens and perplexing questions. I would discuss my philosophies, frustrations, and fears and inadequacies with Him, knowing that He possessed the perfect ability to respond to me in a way that would meet my needs specifically. I would ask Him about "gray areas"—how to be humble while resolute, when to be angry and when to set anger aside, or how to know where my will ends and His will begins. His answers would be perfectly balanced. He would be the epitome of the perfect friend. He would know when to question me and when to sit back and listen. He would know when to confront and when to lend support.

As I think about how this imaginary discussion with Jesus Christ would impact my life afterward, I am certain that much more than just His words and philosophies would stand out in my mind. No doubt the greatest impression that would be left by this encounter would be His presence. Although the words He spoke would prompt new thoughts, I would be most drawn to Him not by His words but by His mannerisms. An unforgettable image of a man who loved as no one else could, one who understood as no one else before, and one who projected a calm confidence and infinite inner peace would be stamped on my mind.

I am anticipating the day when I arrive in heaven and will be able to have such an encounter with Jesus. But at this point in life, I am satisfied to communicate with Him through prayer and the study of His revealed Word. In doing so, I can still grasp the essence of His presence.

---

*As we demonstrate the presence of
Christ in our own lives, our efforts
to find inner peace become complete.*

Although Jesus ascended to heaven having accomplished in the flesh what He intended, He left behind Spirit-controlled men and women to carry on the task of giving individuals glimpses of His character. Although no individual is able at this time to interact with Jesus in the flesh, born-again believers can be His earthly instruments and can communicate the person of Jesus Christ to those who are seeking. Through us, others can come to know Him and His message of spiritual wholeness. In His last earthly statement Jesus said to His followers, "You shall receive power when the Holy Spirit has come upon you; and you shall be My witnesses" (Acts 1:8).

This has major implications for the Christian who has come to terms with himself in the Lord. Although we each will have the ultimate desire to feel the personal satisfaction of being loved by Christ, our overriding goal will be to show Christ to those who are still searching. This will be accomplished not just by what we say but by who we are. As we demonstrate the presence of Christ in our own lives, our efforts to find inner peace become complete.

Scott struggled for years with problems of guilt, inferiority, and fear of rejection. His lifestyle of rebellion and immorality only confounded his problems with the debilitating emotions. In therapy, Scott disclosed many of the reasons for his emotional and behavioral problems. His background had been instrumental in the development of his insecurity and maladaptive ideas. He needed to set aside the guiding thoughts that led to his various personal struggles, choosing instead to focus on the truths of God's Word. In time, Scott experienced a transformation. He became calm and confident a majority of the time, and his behavior was more responsible than before.

SEVEN TRAITS OF CHRIST'S RELATIONAL STYLE

Respect
Empathy
Warmth
Submission to God
Objectivity
Confidence
Genuineness

Asked by his counselor to recall how he had been able to make such significant changes, Scott said, "As we would share ideas and talk about my emotions, I could see in your eyes that you really cared for me. I knew it was real. And when I would think about the thoughts that God wanted me to have, your concern for me made me know it was OK to accept God's concern as real, too." Scott's reply reflected that the theoretical aspect of counseling had taken a back seat to the experiential aspect.

The counselor's attitude toward Scott was vitally important to his process of making peace with himself. After all, Scott needed a knowledge of God's Word as it applied to the many struggles he had encountered. But the vehicle that carried this knowledge into Scott's heart and mind was the therapeutic relationship. As the counselor was able to project the presence of Jesus, Scott became awakened to the power of His truths. It was when the love of Christ was experienced that the thoughts of Christ were integrated into his mental processes.

In preceding chapters we have examined two of the prerequisites to finding inner peace: (1) discovering who we are, and (2) understanding why we do what we do. At this point we will explore the third ingredient: yielding our lives to God. Specifically, this means that through prayer and concentration we can learn to relate to others in a style consistent with the character of Christ. Since Christ was the model of a life pleasing to God, we will examine several of Christ's traits. By developing these traits, we will deepen our ability to love and minister to those we encounter.

RESPECT

An ultimate goal in personal relationships is to show the love of God. We enhance the peace within us by acts of giving, and in the process we can be used as instruments of God.

Ask yourself, *What is the greatest gift I can give to another human?* Although we may be prone to think in terms of material offerings, we must remind ourselves that we are spiritual beings created for relationships. With that in mind, we could conclude that the most meaningful thing we can give another human being is the gift of respect.

Respect can be defined as a caring concern and an unconditional regard for others. It is the recognition of a person's worth. The individual who offers respect demonstrates the love of God. And the recipient feels esteemed and valued. The respectful person has no desire to pass judgment, preferring instead to freely allow others to be who they are. It is consistent with the love expressed by Christ: "Come to Me, all who are weary and heavy-laden, and I will give you rest. Take My yoke upon you and learn from Me, for I am gentle and humble in heart" (Matthew 11:28–29).

An individual's ability to show consistent respect for others is contingent upon his own relationship with God.

Offering respect to others is not always natural, even for the mature Christian. Because we are each still in the flesh, we are susceptible to flaws in our abilities to show love.

Several years ago I counseled a man who was repeatedly involved in the sexual abuse of children. Although he said that he wanted to change, he was unable to show signs of remorse. He seemed matter-of-fact in his descriptions of his past behaviors. As I listened to this man's misdeeds, I found it difficult to feel respect for him. However, as our sessions continued, I realized that he lacked any experience of real love. His family history was full of violence. I realized that if I did not show positive regard for him, he could spend the rest of his life knowing nothing but emptiness and aggravation.

Setting aside my feelings, I let the Holy Spirit use me to communicate that he was valued by God. I began to genuinely care for his spiritual and psychological well-being, and it showed on my face and in my tone of voice. I reasoned that if God could love me and desire fellowship with me in spite of my sinfulness, surely I could follow God's lead and exhibit the same toward this hurting man. In time he told me that no one had ever treated him with as much care as I had, and it amazed him because I knew so many negative things about him. My response was to thank God for letting me be used to show His care.

An individual's ability to show consistent respect for others is contingent upon his own relationship with God. Outside the love of God we each have biases and prejudices that create conditional regard for others. Our natural predisposition is to love only those who live within the scope of our own human capacity for acceptance. But those who seek to be Spirit-controlled can determine to set self's prejudices aside, allowing God's unconditional love to be supernaturally communicated. We can learn to operate not on our own ability but on the ability derived from the indwelling presence of Christ. We can echo Paul's statement in Galatians 2:20: "I no longer live, but Christ lives in me" (NIV).

It is impossible to overestimate others' need for Christian love and respect. Because we were each created by God for relational love, it is the deepest need that can be known. And because our sinful world is flawed in its ability to give love, respect is a gift not given with sufficient frequency. As we learn to show respect to those who come into our lives, we communicate, "I truly want God's best for you. You are valued and significant." As this is done, we demonstrate that we are at peace with ourselves and that we want others to experience peace too.

EMPATHY

John 11:35 is the shortest verse in the Bible: "Jesus wept." Some people had approached Jesus with the news that His close friend Lazarus was dying. When they asked Jesus to hurry to Lazarus's side, He did not rush, knowing that God was going to work a miracle. By the time Jesus neared Lazarus's home in Bethany, Lazarus had been dead four days. Outside the village, Jesus greeted Lazarus's sister Martha, who then summoned her sister, Mary. As Mary approached Jesus, she broke into tears, expressing tremendous anguish. As her emotions flowed, Jesus is said to have been deeply moved in spirit, becoming troubled. It was then that Jesus joined Mary in her tears. Jesus did not cry because He felt helpless in the circumstances; He had already predicted that He would miraculously heal Lazarus. Rather, His outpouring of emotions occurred because He had empathized with Mary, and He felt her hurt and her brokenness as if it were His own. He was so involved in her communication that He had completely absorbed the essence of her spirit.

Empathy creates a bond between people and builds a spirit of cohesiveness enabling them to attend to each other's words and feelings. *Empathy* can be defined as a vicarious experiencing of the thoughts, emotions, and perceptions of another individual that creates a powerful understanding of that person's perspective. It includes an awareness and a sensitivity to that individual's unique inner struggles.

For empathy to be a significant factor in relationships, it is not enough that it be *felt;* it must also be clearly *communicated.* That is, it is not enough for an empathizer to merely understand the other person's unique perspective; the understanding must be openly spoken or demonstrated before empathy is complete. This communication can be transmitted verbally in a reflective statement, such as "When people ignore you, a deep hurt develops, and it must cause you to feel very disillusioned." Or perhaps the empathy can be communicated with a caring, knowing facial expression or nod of the head. As empathy is communicated, the recipient feels attached to one who is capable of comprehending his struggles, and consequently he becomes a trusted friend whose suggestions, opinions, and reflections are taken seriously.

---

*We cannot experience true
inner peace until we give of
ourselves in understanding others.*

The process of establishing empathy can begin literally in the first minute of contact. As an individual shares personal feelings or experiences, the empathizer can make it his task to feel and communicate something of that person's uniqueness in relation to the subjects expressed. Clarifying questions can be asked, such as "How did it feel to know that your supervisor cited you as being the one employee he could always count on?" Identifying statements may be offered: "As I put myself in your shoes, I can only imagine how bewildering it must feel to be so alone." Restatement of the individual's words can be given: "So when your husband speaks rudely, all you know to do is to sit tight and keep your mouth closed." Throughout the interaction process, these and other statements can be consistently expressed as a means of letting the individual know that his point of view is understood.

Concentration is vital in establishing this trait. The empathizer must be someone who has resolved that his own sinful pride will not get in the way of understanding the other person. That is, the empathizer does not want to have an "agenda" that creates impatience and the desire to control. Nor does the empathizer need to be preoccupied with other matters, such as mentally planning the day's schedule, worrying about making the "right" response, or making judgments about that person's character. The overwhelming desire to feel with the individual in his expressions and experiences is the major factor that causes empathy to be genuinely transmitted.

The necessity of empathy in our lives underscores the fact that we were created by God for relationships, and we cannot experience true inner peace until we give of ourselves in understanding others. The need in those around us is so universal that the one who does not empathize is missing a basic element of living. In early childhood development, emotional attachment must first be established before a child can integrate intellectual stimulation. And in the adult years, this sequence is still necessary. Consequently, one's effort to find peace is not likely to be successful until the ability to place self into the shoes of others is consistently practiced.

WARMTH

Almost every person can dredge up memories of a school teacher whose disposition was as sour as the day was long.

That teacher may have made it a point to teach her lessons thoroughly, but her lack of warmth negated the possibility that what was learned would be enthusiastically recalled after her days of giving examinations were completed.

Warmth is a necessary trait. We may be intelligent in a wide range of subjects, but, if we are detached, the relationship will never get off the ground. Warmth communicated in the spoken word, tone of voice, and facial expression is an adjunct to the traits of respect and empathy. A warm demeanor reveals the characteristics inside a person that might otherwise go unnoticed.

Mark 10:13–16 records how young children are brought to Jesus so that He might touch them. Christ must have been enamored by the children's innocence. Yet while this was happening His disciples rebuked the people and told them to leave Jesus alone. Jesus responded, "Permit the children to come to Me; do not hinder them." As much as anything else, I'm sure Jesus was hurt to think that He would be deprived of the chance to share Himself with little ones who absorbed His warmth like sponges. In fact, this passage reiterates that He then took the children in His arms and blessed them.

Imagine the gentleness exuding from Christ as He was swarmed by His young admirers. No doubt the parents went away that day having learned a prime lesson in the art of loving. They had seen how the man of peace was naturally at ease with children. His character was filled with a warmth that attracted the most sensitive and intuitive of people. Jesus' warm demeanor was a vehicle that carried His love to the heart of the recipient.

When warmth is present, anxiety is reduced.

Warmth can be defined as a comfortable feeling of well-being and compassion conducive to the establishment of friendship and relational security. As warmth is expressed, personal relationships develop that convey closeness and caring.

The recipient senses that it is acceptable to expose his deepest thoughts and feelings, knowing the atmosphere offers acceptance and gentleness.

Some individuals desperately need a caring interchange from someone who has mastered Christian warmth. One woman came to my office on the heels of a divorce, proclaiming that she hated all men. Both her father and her husband were abusive. I realized that this woman needed to be treated tenderly. Although I was interested in her thoughts, I also knew that she could not change her ideas without some experience to validate what I wanted her to learn. After a few individual sessions I encouraged her to join in group therapy, knowing it would offer her a more natural experience of warm interchanges than individual counseling. When she was ready to terminate counseling, she specifically recalled her early statement about hating all men. With a sigh of relief she stated that she had new hope because of her experiences with compassionate men. It never ceases to amaze me how people change as a result of kindness more than as the result of brilliant concepts or theories.

When people seek to establish relationships, it is possible they may feel weak, overwhelmed, or highly frustrated. Consequently they need a relationship with an individual who does not add stress. When warmth is present, anxiety is reduced, and eventually one begins to feel confident in the relationship, knowing that it offers safety and comfort. Because the experience of God's presence is essential to relational growth, it can be accomplished when an atmosphere consistent with His care is fostered.

SUBMISSION TO GOD

Since inner peace is derived from the belief that God's Word offers the ultimate truth to our emotional struggles, an integral part of maintaining that peace is to practice genuine submission to God. That means, foremost, that the believer knows about God not merely in an intellectual manner but through a personal experience. He will declare publicly that he has voluntarily decided to set aside self's preferences for sin with a commitment to allow Jesus Christ to be Savior and Master. This specifically implies that when the believer relates to others, there will be an understanding that he has a deep allegiance to the will of God. Others will notice that a special ingredient is present in his life.

What was the most excruciating emotional experience in Jesus' life? Some might choose His trial or His agony on the cross. But while those events certainly created anguish, I would choose Jesus' time of prayer in the Garden of Gethsemane immediately prior to His arrest. It was then that He was praying so fervently that sweat like drops of blood poured from Him. He even asked His Father that, if He would will it, the impending task might be removed from Him. But He also said, "Yet not My will, but Thine be done" (Luke 22:42). It was this attitude that carried Him through the mock trial and the humiliation of being made sin on the cross in our behalf.

Submission to the authority of the Father was a cornerstone element in the peace that Jesus Christ experienced while in the flesh. If questioned or ridiculed by crowds, He maintained composure knowing that His inner stability came from being connected with the Father. If faced by Satan and his temptations, His submissiveness carried Him through. When weary because of His disciples' lack of faith, He stayed patiently by them because of His awareness of His mission for the Father. In all that He did, a submissive spirit permeated His being, which then influenced His manner of interacting with others. He was at peace with Himself because He knew His position before the Father.

Submission to God does not
relegate women to a doormat position,
nor does it make mice out of men.

Using a certain amount of creative license, we might say that the word *submission* is composed of two parts: "sub" (which when used as a prefix means "beneath") and "mission." Viewing the word in this way, we might say that *submission* means "being on a mission for the one we are beneath." Our lives are to be understood as a mission for God whatever our role may be.

Each day in my counseling office I am faced with individuals who have the knowledge of God's Word but lack inner peace because the element of submission to God is missing. Many of these people have professed belief in Christ as Savior, but it is a belief of their intellect, not of their entire being. Consequently, anxiety, anger, impatience, and the like are regular ingredients in their personality. There has not been a complete letting go of the controls of one's emotions. Subservience to God occurs only when convenient.

I am struck by the reaction of many people (Christian and non-Christian) to the word *submission.* It arouses contempt from people who believe submissiveness cheats them of their personhood. Many women feel belittled when a speaker suggests that a submissive spirit is a vital ingredient in healthy family relations or in church organizations. They assume that this insinuates that they will become nonentities. Many men bristle when it is suggested that they too should develop a heart of a servant, setting self aside and acquiescing to an authority higher than themselves.

Yet if I correctly understand the character of Christ, submission to God does not relegate women to a doormat position, nor does it make mice out of men. On the contrary, as we submit to God we attain a greater status. By submitting to God we attain an identity and purpose that is far superior to anything this world can offer.

A man we'll call Thomas sought counseling for periods of depression. Thomas performed well in his profession, and when his performances were at their peak he felt happy and content. But when he hit a snare that led to struggle and failure, the depression would appear. For years his emotions were like a swinging pendulum, alternating between feelings of success and defeat. I challenged Thomas to evaluate the commitment that he had made to God ten years earlier. Although Thomas had publicly professed Christ as Savior and had grown in his knowledge of Scripture, he did not feel that his life was truly a mission for God. As we discussed what full submission to God implied, Thomas acknowledged his need to reconstruct his ideas about success. He realized that lasting success—and its subsequent feeling of contentment—comes not through performing perfectly but through living in daily awareness that he is a representative of God whose purpose is to show his world God's love.

Many individuals casually seek an affair or a divorce because they have lost their love for their mates. Knowing that this is not what God wants them to do, they do it anyway, and inevitably they reap the emotional consequences. Individuals with homosexual leanings go against God's natural laws and succumb to a lifestyle of sin. Drug and alcohol abusers pollute their bodies with unnatural substances. Other individuals engage in poor communication practices that are recognizably in contradiction to biblical principles.

When we submit to God's guidance, we not only are recognizing His supreme authority and holiness, but we are laying claim to the benefits and natural consequences of an alignment with that which is truly good. So rather than being something that detracts from a person's identity, submission to God adds to our quality of life.

OBJECTIVITY

A person at peace with self is characterized by objectivity. *Objectivity* can be defined as being uninfluenced by emotion or prejudice to the extent that another person's revelation does not adversely affect the ability to relate with logic and fairness. In contrast, the individual who lacks objectivity is easily disturbed or offended, which creates an inability to get beyond the superficial aspects of an individual's communications, succumbing instead to one's own biases and frailties. Whereas the nonobjective person becomes ensnared by another's struggle, the objective individual is able to empathize with others' emotions and experiences without the loss of personal composure and reasoning.

Knowing and accepting the truth about who we are as sinners can keep us from being shocked by exposures to another's imperfections.

    Some time ago a man was dragged into my counseling office by his wife, who had caught him in an adulterous relationship. The man obviously did not want to be there, and within minutes he was pointing his finger at me, telling me that I was not going to make him succumb to my Christians beliefs. After a five-minute tirade, during which time he used profanity and derogatory language, I calmly told him that I was glad to know how he felt about counseling since such knowledge would assist me in communicating with him. Fully expecting me to be just as angry as he was, this man was confused by my response. Although the man wanted to fight with me, I remained understanding and unoffended. That objectivity gave him an illustration of a rational style of communicating. Several sessions later he thanked me for being patient rather than offended toward his emotional explosion.

    Before a single conversation occurs between ourselves and others, we must remind ourselves that every person alive is or has been afflicted with a wide variety of stresses and strains. No one is immune due to the fact that we live in a depraved world. Consequently, before an emotional outburst occurs or an unflattering experience is shared, the objective listener will do well to brace for the unexpected. All humans are capable of untold sins, and we must recognize that no individual is going to live without some difficulty with matters of sin. Even the individuals who outwardly appear to be fine Christians can have significant struggles with the flesh. Knowing and accepting the truth about who we are as sinners can keep us from being shocked by exposures to another's imperfections.

A classic example of personal objectivity is Jesus' encounter with the Samaritan woman in John 4. That the woman was at the well during midday indicated that she had experienced interpersonal problems—otherwise she would have drawn water early in the morning with the rest of the women. In her initial conversation with Jesus she was curt, but her mood soon turned to curiosity as Jesus spoke about living water. When Jesus mentioned her husband, she was defensive, and, when He revealed that He was aware of her five previous marriages as well as her current adulterous relationship, she was awestruck. Throughout the conversation the woman was confused about what she should think. But Jesus maintained His objectivity because He had resolved to be unshaken by her personal struggles. In His mind He had ideas about how best to speak with this woman, and He proceeded according to those well-conceived thoughts rather than reacting to her emotional instability.

In the same way the person at peace with self can maintain personal composure by having a sound knowledge that "all have sinned and fall short of God's glory." Knowing this, a balance can be struck between emotional involvement with others and intellectual detachment.

The applications of this trait are numerous. Think, for example, of the fewer arguments married couples would have if they learned to objectively understand the strengths and weaknesses of one another without feeling the need to react to the inevitable flaws. Or imagine how a parent could maintain a more consistent composure if he recognized that his children will make mistakes by virtue of the fact that they are mere mortals who cannot be expected to handle all circumstances with perfection and maturity. Or picture the difference in work settings or church or social gatherings if we each would rationally acknowledge that differences are a part of groups and that mistakes are bound to occur. The emotional calm that is a part of gaining personal awareness and understanding could be maintained for rewarding lengths of time.

CONFIDENCE

Jesus was not an insecure person; in fact, He had tremendous confidence in Himself. He was not prone to cowering when someone attempted to corner Him with loaded questions. On the contrary, when He spoke, He exuded authority and certainty in a manner that astounded crowds (see Matthew 7:28–29). Knowing who He was and what He was about, Jesus Christ was able to maintain a consistency of inner confidence. The person who has made peace with himself can have this trait, too.

---

*By definition, confidence does
not include arrogance or a
desire for dominance.*

The level of personal confidence is extremely important to the lifestyle of a composed individual. Confidence can be three-directional: toward God, toward self, and toward others. These three directions can be further expanded: (1) God has revealed all the necessary standards for proper living in a way that can be clearly understood by each person; (2) as we appeal to the power and direction of God, God will supply us with the ability to do His will; and (3) others can have faith in us as they realize that our lives are solidly grounded in a resolute demeanor.

The *confidence of a contented individual* can be defined as faith and assurance in one's personal abilities, based on the knowledge that the Holy Spirit will guide one's efforts with discernment. It is this confidence that enables a person to project himself as one who can be trusted and believed. By definition, confidence does not include arrogance or a desire for dominance. Instead, it assumes a lack of fear or embarrassment and the presence of composure and certainty.

Perhaps one of the greatest repercussions of an individual's confidence is the hope it can instill in those near us. Family, friends, and acquaintances often look for someone to give signals that say, "When difficulties arise, we can handle them." They are looking for a person who offers hope. And when hope is present, those people's minds can be awakened to optimism and expectancy for the prospect of successful relationships. Without it, we can feel pessimistic and unmotivated to make the effort required in relationships. The confidence exuded by the person at peace with himself can subtly but powerfully transmit the message that God's strength is present, and it can thereby create an atmosphere conducive to healthy relationships.

I vividly recall hearing a public testimony given by a man named James, who had once been caught in the throes of depression for several months. In his testimony James told how he had experienced lifelong problems of insecurity and passivity. Not feeling competent to take a stand for his most basic needs and desires, he had stumbled through an unstable career and through an unsteady marriage. He readily admitted that his childhood had not prepared him for the rigors of adult life, and as each year passed he became more prone to depression.

Feeling hopeless, James sought professional Christian counseling. He stated his apprehension about opening up to a complete stranger. "I felt like I was disrobing myself in broad daylight, leaving myself psychologically naked to this man. I'd never done anything like it before." As the initial session unfolded, the counselor outlined some of the key issues in this man's life that could profitably be explored. James's eyes lit up as he said, "After I told the counselor my story and he shared his initial impressions, he looked straight at me and said, 'You know, if we both are committed to the work to be done here, you can change.' Imagine that! He told me I could change. Nobody had ever said that to me before. I was absolutely elated!"

More than astounding theories and insights, James had been looking for a reason to hope. And he found it the moment the counselor had expressed a confidence in their ability to make things happen. Literally, this single factor had been the key that spawned a readiness in him to challenge his thinking patterns. The counselor had become a significant model for James, and his belief in God's ability to work in them became the springboard for a successful series of sessions that taught him a new way of life.

By means of a calm, assured manner the message had been communicated: "There is no problem so overwhelming that it will totally defeat you. With the help of God, things don't have to be the way they are." James's illustration shows that the counselor's sense of confidence was not merely a self-contained trait. It was contagious.

GENUINENESS

So far we have discussed how several characteristics can be present when a person has come to have the presence of Christ within. But each of the traits discussed will have an empty ring if it is not also accompanied by genuineness. Although this trait is intangible, its presence can be readily discerned by those who are observing our behaviors for cues to signal that we can be trusted. Whether we like it or not, other people may be skeptical when we act respectful or empathetic or confident. So, consciously or subconsciously, they will be looking for verifications that speak of the genuineness of our actions.

Genuineness is defined as being worthy of belief. The genuine individual lives without pretense, free from the burden of facades and unnecessary performances. A composure is present that communicates, "I am at peace with myself, and I have contentment." No particular effort is made to "sell" oneself because the genuine person is willing to let others formulate their opinions as they will. Consequently, others sense that when words are spoken they are sincere; when care is expressed, it is from the heart.

Several years ago I spoke with a minister who made the decision to leave the pastorate to pursue a career in business. He told me that his heart had never been committed to "professional ministry." For several years he had struggled with the many demands placed on him. He had to force patience. He was frequently discouraged when people did not grow spiritually at the rate he wished. Often his mind would wander as someone recounted a personal experience, and he was not certain if the encouragement he offered was of much help. He explained, "I felt like I was acting in a role that should have been filled by someone other than me." He had rightly concluded that he was not a good candidate for the pastorate. Although he was a fine Christian who knew much about the Bible, he did not have that extra measure of genuineness enabling him to pastor in a believable way.

Most people we encounter have been exposed to relationships that are anything but genuine.

Genuineness presupposes several factors. First, one's Christian lifestyle must be more of a desire than a duty. To be genuinely credible, the individual must have the deep conviction in his heart that God's love is a specific preference placed on his heart by God Himself. Such things as kindness and patience are not practiced because of Christian obligation but because of a fervor to live in such a manner. Second, the genuine individual is one who has thought about his beliefs on a broad range of subjects and is capable of expressing convictions and preferences that are not merely theoretical or borrowed, but they are one's own. Third, there is a well-integrated conception about the profoundness of knowing God's holiness and living with an awareness of it. The individual understands that he is a spiritual being first, and the ability to lovingly relate to another is accomplished as he becomes attuned to his own position before God. Fourth, the individual is aware of his own tremendous ability to sin, resulting in real humility that causes him to sidestep the temptation to be superior, choosing to speak *with* others rather than *to* them. Fifth, the individual is not controlled by fear and defensiveness but is open to feedback and is willing to make himself vulnerable. In doing so, he sets an example worthy of following and becomes a friend to those in need. Then, finally, there is a willingness to communicate immediate feelings and reactions in an unrehearsed manner, modeling healthy communication for others.

Most people we encounter have been exposed to relationships that are anything but genuine. They have known the fear of having to be guarded in the expression of hurt feelings or controversial thoughts, and they have been exposed to hundreds of circumstances requiring "proper" performances. They have felt rejection when flaws have been revealed to friends or family members, consequently creating a hesitancy in the acceptance of themselves and of others. It is predictable that most people will welcome a relationship that not only allows realness but encourages it. We can become living illustrations of wholeness that will inspire others toward openness and authenticity in relationships.

There are times when tactful self-disclosures can augment the atmosphere of genuineness. Rather than presenting oneself as a stodgy individual who is beyond problems, it can be helpful to tactfully expose our own humanness. I specifically recall the shock in one woman's face when I told her I could identify with her feelings of futility when her children were disobedient. When I told her we had similar moments in our household, she quickly retorted, "I know you don't have any problems at your house; you just can't." Chuckling, I told her that our goal can be to handle our struggles as they appear rather than hoping they will go away forever. By my simple self-disclosure I let her know that I could personally identify with her emotions while also having a well-conceived plan to face them.

In summary, finding peace with oneself cannot be considered complete until there is also an ability to respond to others in a manner that illustrates the presence of God's guiding hand. As we share His love with those nearest us, we experience the satisfaction of knowing that we are consistent with His character.

12

COMMUNICATION SKILLS AND TECHNIQUES

Each of us has been in the awkward circumstance of not knowing what to say or do. Think for a moment about your first date. Do you remember how you fidgeted for the right words at the front door? And can you recall the self-consciousness you felt when your manners proved to be barbaric at best? It's humbling just to think about it.

I wish I could promise that awkward communication would be nonexistent once we reach adulthood. But you already know better than that. We have no guarantee at the beginning of the day that each interpersonal exchange will proceed without a hitch. The majority of us simply have not been trained to communicate smoothly in every circumstance. And even those of us who have received training in communication skills will sheepishly admit that we frequently stray from our textbook knowledge. Simply stated, relating to others does not come automatically and effortlessly. It takes discipline!

Up to this point, we have attempted to understand ourselves both psychologically and spiritually in an effort to find the road to peace. It is invaluable to know how sin influences human nature and how Scripture teaches us to overcome our struggles. And it is therapeutic to understand how our family background has influenced our patterns of emotions. But we can't stop there if we desire to come full circle to a life of contentment. We each have a need to structure our communications in such a way that our interchanges can be fully rewarding. This is particularly true as it relates to our ability to communicate with the people closest to us.

When we attend to another's words, feelings, and expressions, we create an atmosphere conducive to sharing God's grace.

In relating to those closest to us, we are called upon to communicate in ways that illustrate and enhance emotional composure. Consequently, it would be helpful to contemplate the skills and techniques that are an intricate part of knowing how to relate more effectively and deeply with others. As we learn to incorporate loving communication into our lifestyles, we continue in the effort to yield ourselves to God's guidance. In conjunction with the traits listed in chapter 11 (respect, empathy, warmth, and so on), these communication tools can help us express God's love to those around us. Eight skills can change the course of our lives if we will let them.

ATTENDING

We must begin by learning to attend to the thoughts, feelings, and perceptions of others. *Attending* can be defined as directing careful concentration toward someone. It is expressed through eye contact, alertness, facial expressions, and appropriate reactions. It provides tangible evidence of our genuine care for another. When we attend to another's words, feelings, and expressions, we create an atmosphere conducive to sharing God's grace. The person we are with begins to think, *I am being taken seriously, and as a result I will be all the more committed to building up this relationship.* The significance of this can be phenomenal.

I can still recall a very early experience in my clinical internship that taught me the value of attending. A woman had come to our clinic distraught because her husband had abandoned her and her infant son. She was full of emotion and desperately seeking someone who could understand her plight. When I asked her to tell me her experiences, she poured out her soul with tears and anguish. For most of the session, I let her talk, and I expressed concern and understanding for her feelings. My voice was soft and my heart was sincere. She went into a long discourse about the trials of her marriage. It was clear that she was in need of a good listening ear. As our session came to a close, however, I had an unsettled feeling because we had not taken the time to discuss in depth some ideas that I thought would help her in her emotional struggles. Here I was, this brilliant graduate student with great insights to give, and I didn't have the time to expound on my wisdom!

Eight Communication Skills

Attending
Soliciting
Active listening
Clarification
Silence
Confrontation
Self-disclosure
Interpretation

As she stood to leave she told me that it had literally been years since anyone had taken the time to show so much concern for her. She had been so starved for attention that the very fact that I showed interest was therapeutic. My attentiveness proved far more valuable than I had realized. I learned a lesson that day about the value of truly tuning in to a person's needs.

Everything we do communicates something. No act is devoid of meaning. We may assume that relationships succeed when we share pleasant events with, or know significant facts about, someone. But true bonding does not occur until the other person receives clear and consistent communication that says "You're important to me." This is done with good eye contact, a knowing nod, inquisitive remarks, a pleasant demeanor, and a show of appropriate concern. By noticing the subtle and obvious cues of friends, we set the stage for genuine communication. The other person begins to feel that there is a purpose in relating, and he gains affirmation of his self-worth.

It must be emphasized that attending is not merely a ploy that can be easily faked. Nor is it a skill that can be taught from a textbook. In order to communicate genuine interest, we must have genuine, God-given compassion for the needs of those around us. Anything short of that would eventually be exposed as insincere.

Although soliciting involves asking
questions, it is much more than that.

By attending to the expressions and needs of others, we can learn to overcome our preoccupation with self and the pride that leads us into sin. As we practice attending, we practice humility and follow Christ's example of giving esteem to others.

SOLICITING

Most of us have fantasized about relationships that are open and honest. Yet in reality we find that much of our communication is structured and phony. Most of us won't let down our public veneers without some prodding. I recall conferring with a woman who was curious to know if I had made any headway at all in private discussions with her husband. Although I have ethical guidelines that restricted me from sharing our conversations, I did tell her that we experienced some true soul-searching interchanges. Shocked, she told me that she rarely heard him say anything of a personal nature, so she was eager to know how I had pulled any self-revelations from him. "Simple," I told her. "I asked him."

Kicking around theoretical ideas or facts and figures is not the same thing as communicating. In close relationships, we want to structure our communication in ways that encourage personal interchange. That is part of what makes relationships successful. If we discuss ideas without revealing what lies inside us, our communication becomes impersonal. Our discussions become more profitable when we know the uniqueness of the other person. But because some individuals are hesitant to boldly blurt out their deepest thoughts or because they may not know which self-disclosures are going to be accepted, we may need to solicit the things that will enhance the personal dimension of a relationship.

Soliciting is defined as a method of questioning that encourages another to openly share feelings, experiences, and ideas in a way that leads us to better know that person. It enables the solicitor to more fully understand the meaning inherent in that person's behaviors, emotions, and communications. Soliciting brings personal enlightenment, because it creates an atmosphere that aids the process of self-discovery. Although soliciting involves asking questions, it is much more than that. It can also include expressions of interest in matters close to another's heart or of confusion regarding vague subjects or of encouragement to continue with communication that is incomplete. Let's keep in mind that soliciting is entirely different from being snoopy, since its goal is to create greater intimacy rather than to acquire juicy tidbits for gossip or manipulation.

I must admit that when I don my counselor's hat, soliciting is a far easier task than it is when I am in an environment where less heavy subjects are explored. You see, many counselees would be surprised, perhaps even disappointed, if I did not seek to ascertain disclosures that supersede normal relationships. But this is not necessarily the case in more normal settings. Even so, I believe that many, if not most, individuals would be willing to let themselves be more deeply known if a genuine, nonthreatening opportunity were presented to them.

Examples of solicitation abound. You can verbally recall what a person told you the day before and ask follow-up questions. You may read a person's mood and make a statement regarding it. You can share how interested you are in a topic and ask for input from the other person. You can be willing to introduce a sensitive subject (such as an inquiry about a person's problems with a teenaged son) and ask how the matter is going.

We must be careful not to use solicitation as a predetermined program or simply a means to an end. Instead, we should see it as a way to communicate genuine interest in the other person and to build confidence in the relationship. When we communicate openly, our relationships gain depth. We will find greater rewards by risking vulnerability than by hiding behind masks of phoniness.

The extent of our soliciting will vary depending on whether we are among family members, friends, or casual acquaintances. But the mechanics are the same. Whether you are speaking as a wife to a husband at the dinner table or as a church member to a visitor, you can show interest in the person by soliciting their thoughts and feelings. Without being pushy or presumptive, you gently create an atmosphere that says "I care about you."

ACTIVE LISTENING

After we have solicited information from someone, it is important that we listen to his feelings, thoughts, and experiences. The role of active listening in communication cannot be overstated. Without this element, relationships cannot be expected to mature. Each individual has a unique combination of feelings, thoughts, and perceptions, and the listener needs not only to hear the words spoken but to gain a perspective of the other person's uniqueness. That can be done only by taking time for contemplation.

Active listening is not the same as sitting quietly while waiting for a turn to speak. Rather, it is hearing and contemplating the messages sent by the speaker. It requires concentration to get into the other person's frame of reference. It is so vital to the outcome of successful relationships that it can be considered essential if personal interactions are to meet their objectives.

> *Success in relationships does not*
> *occur merely as a result of*
> *exchanging interesting information.*

Active listening is distinguished from *mere hearing* when the individual communicates that he or she is listening. For example, if an acquaintance tells you about the sadness she feels as a close friend moves away, you can respond by paraphrasing what you believe to be her feelings: "It leaves you feeling empty, doesn't it?" Or suppose someone suffering from an unwanted divorce says in anger, "It makes me so mad that our family is being disrupted by this nonsense!" You might empathetically add, "I can tell; it's really eating away at you." The speaker then has the satisfaction of feeling heard, and a loving bond is formed in the relationship. Such bonding becomes an important step toward trust and acceptance in the growing relationship.

You will notice that, as you actively listen, you can gain insight into the things that are most pertinent to the speaker— his innermost feelings and struggles as well as his hopes and joys. It leads to empathy—understanding the world from the other person's unique perspective. To that end, you feel you truly *know* the individual in the deepest sense.

Success in relationships does not occur merely as a result of exchanging interesting information. Because we are social creatures, we each have the inborn need to be affirmed and understood. The mind may hold facts about many individuals, but, if I do not interact with their feelings, the information can be labeled as trivia that does little to enhance our relationship.

Listening encourages us to develop Christian compassion in every relationship.

CLARIFICATION

All interpersonal communication is subject to confusion and frustration. After all, we are each unique and will approach events in varying ways. This should not cause alarm; it is just a fact. Consequently, it is not unusual for us to misunderstand those around us. When we are confused by what someone has said, we need to request clarification.

Clarification can be defined as communication that is intended to ease confusion. When clarification is employed properly, vague statements are made more specific, contradictory expressions and feelings are brought into focus and examined, words are applied to feelings that had eluded definition, specific statements replace broad generalities, and examples illustrate key feelings. All of this is done in the interest of bringing ideas, perceptions, and feelings into clear focus.

Some are reluctant to seek clarification because they do not want to appear rude or perhaps ignorant. But, in fact, clarification adds to relational success because it prohibits misunderstandings, thereby averting the possibility of undesirable emotions, like anger or insecurity, to build.

As an example, there are many times when the clarifier will ask the speaker to explain in more detail the meaning of an expression used. Perhaps a friend who tells of tense emotions can be asked to elucidate what happens during these "uptight" times, due to the fact that this expression can mean so many different things. Or a single man who speaks of disillusionment with women may be asked to explain what he means when he says he is disillusioned, particularly if the listener feels this is a term that is being used to veil deeper feelings of anger. Perhaps a marriage partner will state that she and her husband do not communicate well, so the clarifier might ask for an example of a time in which the communication breaks down. In each of these cases, the intent is to draw the problem discussed into clearer focus, which then enables all parties involved to be more certain of the direction they will take in talking with each other.

After several counseling sessions, one woman told me that she had learned to be much more specific in the way she spoke with herself. "You have asked me so many times to clarify what I mean that now I do it automatically to myself. It's getting to the point that I won't let myself get away with making vague complaints that just keep me feeling depressed." She had learned the value of being specific in the way she spoke to herself. She realized that when she spoke in broad generalities or in clichéd terms, she only kept her problems alive.

By knowing when to be silent, we
exhibit sensitivity to another's needs.

As we learn to encourage clarity of expression in our homes and friendships, we can keep minor problems from developing into major ones. For example, have you ever misinterpreted a friend's silence to mean rejection when in fact the person was merely weary? A clarifying question at such a time could keep anxiety low, preventing an erroneous, perhaps painful, reaction. As we gain proficiency in clarification, we will bring peace to our lives.

SILENCE

There are times when the best thing to say to a friend or family member is nothing at all. Keeping in mind that communication occurs even without the exchange of words, the perceptive communicator recognizes that at times a spoken word can actually detract from the mood of the moment. By knowing when to be silent, we exhibit sensitivity to another's needs. By speaking too quickly or too frequently, we portray our need to maintain control or expose our feelings of discomfort with certain emotions. Examples of times when silence is required may include the following:

- ✔ The individual is steeped in thought, trying to find the right words to express a delicate matter.
- ✔ A very deep and painful emotion is expressed and a response would detract from the mood of the moment.
- ✔ Tears are being shed, and there is a need to let them run their course.
- ✔ The individual is struggling to recollect an important memory from the past that has always been rather blurred.
- ✔ The individual is hesitant and is trying to determine how to "break the ice" in a conversation.

By being silent when necessary, we offer the other person greater freedom of expression in that he is allowed to determine his own course of self-expression. In addition, we are showing patience with him and his feelings. Once we learn to adjust to those feelings, silences can set a mood of comfort and provide a soothing lull in the flow of conversation.

The therapeutic impact of silence was brought home to me in a very powerful way when I was counseling a young man named Philip. Philip had been previously misdiagnosed by another doctor as paranoid schizophrenic. Indeed, he was slow of speech, which made him appear sluggish of mind. But it was clear to me that he had more "on the ball" than he had previously been given credit for.

In one session, he told me that he felt the need to share with me some very delicate experiences of rejection by a close co-worker. He started by saying that he was ashamed of himself for the things that had happened in this relationship. Then he hesitated and stared down at the floor for what seemed to be a long time (probably about two minutes). During this pause I sensed that it would be inappropriate for me to pick up the conversation and move it on to something livelier, so we just sat quietly. Finally, I broke the silence by asking very softly: "Would you like to share your thoughts with me?"

He told me that he had paused because he was trying to decide if he should tell me a delicate piece of information. "Somehow I get the feeling that I can trust you, so I'm going to tell you everything." He then proceeded to tell me that he felt guilty because he had indulged homosexual thoughts toward the rejecting co-worker. Although he had never acted in a homosexual manner, he was very afraid to reveal himself to anyone for fear of what that person might think. (I began to understand why the other doctor had assumed the erroneous diagnosis.) I was firmly convinced as he talked with me that if I had pushed him for information during his moment of silent struggle, Philip would not have opened his soul to me as he did. My silence made him feel that he was not being rushed, nor was he working with a "pushy" counselor. Consequently, he had been able to determine within himself that it was safe to disclose such a delicate problem to me.

---

*Loving confrontation creates
a closeness in a way that
passive acceptance cannot.*

During the course of any heart-to-heart interchange, some thought-provoking ideas may be discussed. So it is quite possible, even desirable, that we will want to take some moments of reflection to become aware of reactions and impressions toward the matters under consideration. Silence offers the availability for this to occur. Meted out in balanced doses, it allows for the process of reflection and self-examination to take root in a significant way.

As we use proper silence, we communicate two things. First, an acceptance of the other person is conveyed. We are illustrating that there is no mold or pattern that the other person must fit. Second, we convey an inner comfort with ourselves. A calm confidence is shown that indicates a flexible, humble spirit. This causes the relationship to flourish since that confidence becomes a bridge for deeper interchanges.

CONFRONTATION

I assume that the person at peace with self has the desire to become intricately involved in others' lives. It is not sufficient for a person to develop self-understanding for the purpose of mere intellectual exercise. And one of the ways to become personally engaged with others is to properly confront when necessary. Loving confrontation creates a closeness in a way that passive acceptance cannot. And because of personality differences and flaws in character, it is a necessary ingredient in healthy relationships. In fact, in Ephesians 4:15, believers are encouraged to speak the truth in love with one another as they grow together in Christ.

Loving confrontation is defined as constructively exposing and examining behavior with the intent of bringing unresolved conflicts into focus. It enables the recipient to incorporate information about self that can help him become more specifically attuned to the needs vital to personal growth. Confrontation is part of the give and take of relationships in that it prompts the individual to consider the impressions and perceptions that his or her behaviors leave with others. It differs from common criticism in that it lacks the aura of judgment, and it does not have any ulterior motives related to coercion.

Successful confrontation requires that the confronter first offer acceptance and objectivity and that the recipient recognize it. When confrontation is made in a judicious manner, great care is given to discern the person's readiness. Before you confront, think carefully about whether the confrontation will be beneficial over the course of time.

Confrontation may be direct or gentle. In the case of someone who has been brazenly sidestepping crucial subjects of discussion, you might say, "You're avoiding the real subject again. Let's get back on track." But in the case of someone's avoiding a sensitive topic due to timidity or guilt, you might begin by saying, "I've noticed something about the way you have responded to this subject. Would you like to hear it?" The keys to productive confrontation are sensitivity and tact. Sensitivity comes as we practice the skill of attending.

The signposts that signal the need for confrontation are (1) improper behavior or (2) denial. In view of this, confrontation is considered a major tool intended to create honest examination of feelings and needs. To illustrate, I recall one woman who sought counseling because her seven-year-old daughter was suffering from recurrent stomach disorders. Her family doctor directed her to counseling to determine what might be corrected in the family style of communication. (This woman was also on the brink of losing her husband due to his feeling of being dominated and browbeaten.) In the first few sessions we discussed key issues, such as her imperative style of communication and her subtle use of passive-aggressive anger. We noted how she had been taught such habits in her own dictatorial family background.

As our sessions unfolded it became increasingly apparent to me that this woman was politely tolerating my observations with no real intentions of making any alterations in her guiding thoughts. Knowing that I needed to "add some spice" to our therapy before she decided it was all an exercise in futility, I confronted her by saying: "I'd like to make an observation. I've been discussing with you some distinctly pertinent issues that are part of the reason for the tension in your life. I detect that you are humoring me, but, because it is not particularly what you want to hear, you are letting our discussions stay in this office. It doesn't appear you are giving serious thought to them away from here. Because of the very delicate and possibly explosive nature of your circumstances, I would strongly encourage you to carefully consider your motives for seeking counseling. If it turns out that we are just spinning our wheels, perhaps we should reconsider the advisability of continued sessions."

At first this woman was taken by surprise. No one had spoken quite so directly to her in a long time. She told me she would think about what I was saying, but truthfully I did not know if she would come back. But sure enough, the next week she returned and told me that my confrontation had made a big impact on her. She began to rethink in earnest the things we had discussed and had concluded that, indeed, she needed to strongly consider the insights we had talked about.

---

*Our ultimate goal in any relationship
is to know and be known.*

Obviously, there are risks inherent in confrontation. The confronter can be misconstrued as being unempathetic or controlling. Also, because timing is such a delicate matter, it could come at a time when the recipient is not ready to respond to it. Consequently, a prerequisite to confrontation is the development of a genuinely caring relationship and a keen understanding of the needs and idiosyncrasies of the individual. It is clear that there were times when Jesus Christ chose to confront individuals, but it must always be understood that He first developed a reputation as a compassionate, aware individual.

In our personal lives, family relations require the most sensitivity in confrontation. Because of daily exposure to one another's differences and quirks, it is easy to take the relationship for granted in such a way that directive communication is offered with little or no compassion. Consequently, it must be stressed that confrontation should not occur until the one confronting is certain that he has already built a reputation for acceptance and that the confrontation is not inconsistent with a message of love.

SELF-DISCLOSURE

Our ultimate goal in any relationship is to know and be known. That is only accomplished when we are willing to expose ourselves to others. In so doing, we become models who encourage authenticity. In a world that promotes phoniness and pretense, it is significant when we learn to openly acknowledge ourselves to another. In doing so, we tend to live more honestly before God as well.

Often, we are prevented from confident self-revelation by two distinct obstacles. First, we may feel that self-disclosure is too risky. Second, we are inexperienced in appropriate ways of sharing ourselves with someone else. When these obstacles exist, we look to others for indications that self-disclosure is safe.

Personal self-disclosure is defined as divulging parts of the deeper, inner self with the intent of exhibiting realness toward those with whom we relate. It does not include the need to "air dirty laundry" before others, but it is a means of letting someone know that we experience the same basic emotions and psychological barriers that they do. It should not be practiced to the extent that it creates an impression of self-preoccupation. It is done to prevent us from remaining a mysterious, unknown entity to others.

As an illustration, I must admit how easily I can identify with the individual who is very performance oriented, to the extent that an overabundance of mental and physical energy is given to life's varied pursuits. Being a doer and an achiever, I can identify with the need for significance and the fear of failure that so frequently thrusts individuals into struggles with impatience or imperative thinking or guilt motivation. Consequently, when I talk with people of like mentality, I will at times share my ability to understand such struggles due to my own past experiences. Without going into excessive detail, I will let these individuals know that I have experienced the tension and impatience that is part of the "performance package." Then, if I ever advise that person to live within a mentality of freedom, willfully choosing kindness over impatience, it is known that I am speaking as one who "has been there." This tactic is much like the style of relating used by the apostle Paul, who would occasionally interject autobiographical information as he witnessed publicly or wrote words of instruction to fellow believers.

One man in particular comes to mind who illustrates the impact of realness in the development of a relationship. After three or four discussions with each other, this man told me, "Before I got to know you, I told myself that I would walk away immediately if you came at me with a bunch of 'Christian theories.' But you seem to speak with me from the heart, and I know that you know what I'm talking about." Keeping my own personal windows open to him made him feel that he could trust me with his innermost needs and feelings. Others feel more capable of acting in a more genuine manner when we willfully (and in proper amounts) become a model for true genuineness. Relationships become less of a plastic exchange of facts and data and more of an attempt to allow authenticity to take root.

INTERPRETATION

Because two people can hear the same sentence and perceive two entirely different meanings, there are times when interpretation is needed. *Interpretation* is defined as discerning the meaning of behavior to the extent that the true significance of that behavior is understandable. Interpretation goes beyond the technique of clarification in that it seeks to discern the definition and significance of external matters. By interpreting, communicators learn to "read between the lines," picking up hidden subtleties in interactions. It is through interpretation that the "meaty" aspects of relating occur.

When friends and family members make interpretive statements to each other, their relationships become fuller.

In order to successfully interpret, it is necessary that the interpreter listen to more than just the words being spoken. Rather, it is necessary to listen for the implicit messages behind the facade of normal communication. The interpreter seeks to read the presence of inner thoughts that the speaker may not be overtly stating. As an example, consider the case of Emily, who had many regular mood swings ranging from euphoria to depression, from love to hate. It became obvious that her extremes in mood were very closely tied to the love and affirmation given or not given by others.

Trying to get at the heart of the matter, I said to her, "On the surface, I hear that you have many changing moods that come and go with the ways people treat you. But beneath the surface, I hear a very lonely person crying out for love. You must have a more-powerful-than-average need to be loved." As soon as I said this, Emily confirmed with tears that I had hit the nail on the head. So rather than speaking immediately to the more superficial aspects of her life, we launched into an interchange regarding her long-standing feelings of loneliness. By interpreting the meaning of her mood swings, our communications developed depth, and Emily felt that she was in the presence of someone truly interested in her real self.

When seeking to make interpretations of behaviors, there are two avenues available. First, the interpreter can state directly, "Here's what I am sensing." This can be a legitimate style of interpretation when the person is unaccustomed to overtly stating his true feelings. The second style of interpretation is to lead the person to read the meaning of his behaviors by asking probing questions. Ultimately, this technique can prove highly profitable since it encourages the individual to think reflectively. It also creates mental strength in that person because the interpreter eventually enables others to become more capable in self-confrontation.

When friends and family members make interpretive statements to each other, their relationships become fuller. There is a lack of pretense and a presence of authenticity. Satisfaction grows because they feel connected to each other.

Unfortunately, we tend to feel inhibited when using this communication technique with our friends and family. After all, think of how paranoid we could become if we thought each of our words and actions was going to be subject to immediate interpretation. Yet close examination of our personal encounters reveals that interpretation can be extremely helpful in creating in-depth interactions.

For example, suppose a husband notices that his wife is in a melancholy mood, moping as she goes about her daily routine. Rather than restating the obvious, he might say, "I suspect you're still disappointed about the argument you had with your mother last night. It must make you feel defeated in your efforts to be kind to her." Going beyond the facts to her feelings, the husband shows a willingness to be involved with his wife in a deep, meaningful way. In this sense, interpretation is not so much an analytical tool as a device that draws another person closer.

13

ULTIMATE HEALING IS A PROCESS

So far we have developed a broad understanding of many of the key issues contributing either to emotional discomfort or personal well-being. At a weekend seminar detailing many of the ideas outlined in this book, a woman told me, "I feel like I'm trying to catch Niagara Falls in a bucket." She related easily to each of the emotions produced by sin. She had experienced many of the side effects of the psychological barriers to personal growth. She yearned to implement the qualities consistent with a growing personality. But it all seemed so overwhelming. Can you relate?

Resolve that you will not pressure yourself to change your emotional and relational problems overnight. It takes a lifetime. And even that is not long enough! A major theme running throughout this book is that change occurs not when we alter a few responses here and there but when we change the *patterns* foundational to who we are. Discovering what lies at the heart of the personality is not an easy task. However, there are some specific steps to take as you come to terms with personal difficulties. Let's examine the five major aspects of growth essential for completing the process of finding inner peace.

FIVE STEPS TO MAKING PEACE WITH YOUR EMOTIONS

1. Identify your various struggles and recognize how and when they manifest themselves.

2. Understand how past experiences influence your current struggles.

3. Acknowledge how your experiences have shaped your current philosophy of life.

4. Recognize how your struggles feed on each other.

5. Develop a growth strategy that converts insight into outward changes in behavior and communication.

STEP 1

Identify your various struggles and recognize how and when they manifest themselves.

The identification process is not as easy as it may appear. Most of us are not trained in clearly recognizing personality features. And even if we are, there can be a powerful defense system at work that keeps us from objectively appraising ourselves. Most of us would rather deny our problems or rationalize them rather than openly declaring that they, in fact, are what they appear to be to others.

For instance, a woman once confronted her husband in my office about his inattentive style of relating with her. She cited several examples of how he had ignored her in days prior and how she felt almost completely shut out from his emotions. He responded by explaining how her impressions were unfounded. He said, "Didn't I tell you how nice you looked last Saturday night when we went out? And didn't I introduce you to the new man at our office when you dropped in last week? You claim I ignore you, but you're just looking for problems that aren't there."

The wife felt deflated and looked to me for support. In the ten or so times that I had counseled with this man, I, too, had found him to be aloof and unexpressive. So I knew her feelings had to have validity. I spoke calmly to the husband: "In relationships, perceptions are extremely important no matter how they may differ with your own thoughts. Because your wife perceives you as insensitive, it would be in your best interest to consider how you could learn from her feedback."

---

*The person who believes he has arrived
at a level of full self-awareness
will be sorely disappointed to discover
that the growth process is ongoing.*

We each have blind spots. We may be able to detect the more obvious personal problems (e.g., loud anger, prolonged depression). But we may need help in identifying the many subtleties in our personality.

Consider another example. A pessimistically minded woman had been told by her family that she seemed bent toward anger. A major part of her counseling was the identification of the many components of anger. For instance, she was prone toward silent judgments of others. She might give cold stares to express displeasure. She was finicky regarding minor household details. Until counseling, she had been unaware that these behaviors were part of her anger system. Once she learned to identify these emotions, she became more inquisitive into the reasons for her anger, and her self-help efforts took off. She later admitted that she was able to change only after she became more skilled in knowing what her problem really was and how it manifested itself.

As we learn to recognize our emotional struggles, we then need to identify the circumstances in which those struggles most commonly surface. For example, a businessman has been exposed to one deadline after another during the day. He is weary of the imperative demands upon him and anger is beginning to grow. On his way home he needs to identify not only his anger, but he needs to acknowledge how he might be susceptible to explode at one of his children. Identifying his vulnerability can be a crucial step in making peace with himself.

Clearly, this tactic of identifying our problems will be used over and over in the course of personal growth. Because of the complexity of our emotions, the potential always exists for finding new ways that our emotional ills can be expressed. The person who believes he has arrived at a level of full self-awareness will be sorely disappointed to discover that the growth process is ongoing. As long as we are on this side of heaven, we have sin to contend with and will never be at a loss for problems to identify.

STEP 2

Understand how past experiences influence your current struggles.

The past is too pertinent to be brushed aside. Because we are creatures of habit, it is relevant for us to comprehend how our current emotional and communication habits originate. Examinations of this nature can lead to an understanding of the year-by-year unfolding of our tendencies. In fact, the apostle Paul on several occasions reflected on his past experiences of anger as he testified about how God had transformed his life (see Acts 22:3–21). We can easily surmise that we are not taught in Scripture to ignore the past; rather, we are to understand it so that we can be freed from it.

Several years ago a reporter asked a well-known national politician to describe the chief traits that qualify a person to hold public office. Wisely, the politician replied that the individual must have the necessary historical frame of reference to make decisions for the present generations. In personal growth, the same premise holds true. An understanding of self becomes complete when the "big picture" is in view.

When considering historical experiences, two extremes should be avoided; obsessively dwelling on history or quickly brushing it aside. The modern emphasis on psychological insight has its place, yet too many people assume that inner healing can only occur *after* many early traumas are recalled and thoroughly dissected. As a backlash to this, some suggest that we should have no worry at all about the past, dealing with current issues only. They may then cite (out of context) Paul's writing of Philippians 3:13, "setting aside the things that are past."

Though we may not be consciously aware of the past's full impact on the present, it wields a powerful influence nonetheless.

Examining the past is helpful to the extent that ongoing trends can be identified and understood, thereby aiding the process of comprehending current circumstances. For instance, a woman recognized that she had many problems of insecurity caused by subtle and unnecessary fears. She made progress as she learned to see her fears in many of her small defensive behaviors. To then help her recognize why these fears could gain a foothold, I encouraged her to explore some historical patterns that led to this trend. She realized that she had deficient love experiences, wondering if she would ever find the approval of each parent. As long as she felt that rejection might come, she hid behind her defensive walls.

We acknowledged that whereas it would have been ideal if her history had provided satisfactory love, she did not have to depend on others for the rest of her life to confer value upon her. She learned that value is a God-given truth. By recognizing her historical pattern, she became keenly aware of the moments when she craved others' approval. Then she reminded herself that her current behavior was probably an overreaction due to those historical deficiencies. She concluded that she did not have to carry past issues with her into each present situation.

Though we may not be consciously aware of the past's full impact on the present, it wields a powerful influence nonetheless. Many experiences combine to create impressions in our minds, affecting us for years down the road. So by gaining knowledge and reflecting on those experiences, we take a step ahead in knowing why we feel as we do today.

STEP 3

Acknowledge how your experiences have shaped your current philosophy of life.

Whether or not we are aware of it, each of us has a philosophy of life that guides our many emotions and behaviors. That philosophy is shaped by innumerable teachings, both experiential and spoken, beginning in childhood and refined in the adult years.

Many people cling to illogical and nonscriptural ideas, not necessarily because they genuinely want to live in error. Rather, they have not been taught to directly confront their guiding philosophies in a manner that causes them to find ideas that could more successfully bring peace of mind. Making true peace with our emotions must include a process of questioning our deepest guiding thoughts.

A common phrase I hear that signals the lack of this self-confrontation is "That's just the way I am." This usually implies a mental laziness that virtually ensures emotional immaturity.

Greg was a middle-aged, "typical," insensitive husband who hid behind the newspaper or stared blankly at the television when his wife preferred real relating. He admitted to me, "I guess I should be more attentive, but that's just the way I am." (That didn't go over well with his wife.) I asked a simple question: "Why?" He looked stunned. He had never contemplated that before.

Reflecting on his past Greg related that his home emphasized the notion of all work and no play. You were a nobody unless you achieved. He threw himself into his work each day, rising by 5:00 and working late each evening. By the time he got home he was worn out, so he gave himself what he deserved: time to do whatever he felt like doing.

"Your guiding philosophy of life," I said, "seems to be that you work until you are ready to drop, collect your paycheck, accumulate a few nice things, then rest up in your free time so you can keep the ball rolling. There seems to be little room for relationships."

"I never thought about it, but I guess that's what I do," he said, stating the obvious.

"Would you consider rearranging your guiding philosophy to downplay the significance of work and give greater emphasis to relating with your family?"

Trying to change our outer behavior without confronting our philosophies of living is like trying to repair a sputtering car by giving it a paint job.

We discussed at length how his guiding thoughts were clearly evidenced in his behavior. And we contemplated how Christianity placed heavy importance on relationships, first with God then with others. Greg concluded that he had been negligent in his husbandly role because he had given little time to sifting out a new philosophy of life.

By examining the guiding thoughts associated with our problems, then making the necessary adjustments, we underscore the notion that transformation involves more than some "how to" adjustments in outer behaviors. Trying to change our outer behavior without confronting our philosophies of living is like trying to repair a sputtering car by giving it a paint job.

Learning new guiding thoughts can be as difficult as learning a foreign language. Even when the language is successfully learned, we still tend to fall back onto the old one. Truly integrating a new language takes years. Likewise, new mental processes can take several years to become first nature. Daily meditation and concentration is essential.

STEP 4

Recognize how your struggles feed on each other.

Often, as people seek counseling, they make the mistake of isolating one or two problems, trying to make sense of these as if they are separate from the rest of their personality. For example, a person may complain of depression, stating that it stems from a background of neglect and abuse. Then they want to focus therapeutically only on the matters that relate overtly to the abuse and the resulting depression.

Our emotions are so closely intertwined that we can safely say that if one emotion is imbalanced many other emotions are probably playing a role in it. Likewise, if we have had a struggle, seemingly, with just one psychological barrier (for instance, the evaluation emphasis), it is probable that we will experience imbalance in the others. As an analogy, the personality is like a finely-tuned engine. If one problem occurs (say the wrong type of fuel is used), it will soon manifest itself throughout the other parts of the engine.

Consider the case of Vicki. She had been divorced five years prior to seeing me, but she still experienced anger because her ex-husband was controlling some leftover financial matters. Though she had hired an attorney who successfully disposed of the financial problems, she sought counseling because of the anxiety this situation had produced.

As is usual in my initial interview, I asked her to talk to me about her family background and her early years of marriage. She told me, "I don't need to get into those subjects because they are irrelevant. My focus is on the anger I feel toward Ron."

Nonetheless, I persisted. "I'd like to have a view of the big picture so that we can address your current problem thoroughly."

Sure enough, I learned that she had a history of many other emotional problems. Her early childhood was filled with insecurity because she had poor reassurances from her parents, particularly her father. Fear and false guilt kept her motivated to do well in her behavior, which might then bring a pat on the back. Socially she carried a secret burden of loneliness. Outwardly she appeared friendly, but inwardly she felt different from her friends. Throughout her adult years she experienced periodic depression and unworthiness because of her husband's rejection. She was jealous and sometimes hostile when her husband was emotionally unavailable.

"Look at the many emotions that have piled up inside yourself through the years," I told Vicki. "Currently you're feeling anxious, but I believe it can be understood as the culmination of many of these other unresolved feelings. The latest haggling with Ron has brought it all out to the front. If you truly want to understand your anxiety, we'll need to figure how these other emotions factor in."

Self-discovery is a many-faceted experience. It takes time to put all the pieces together. In counseling, I help people recognize how one emotion or psychological barrier is likely to spill over into other areas. It can be fascinating to put the pieces of the puzzle together so that you can have a panoramic view of the many components of your emotional system.

STEP 5

Develop a growth strategy that converts insight into outward changes in behavior and communication.

Matthew 7:20 tells us that people are known by their fruit. Whereas the hardest part of personal growth is examining our inner emotions, thought patterns, and attitudes, we need external changes to indicate that our internal awareness is real.

In many respects, the task of converting insight into behavior may appear to be easy. For instance, a complaining person has no problem recognizing that it would be better to have a more encouraging manner of speech. Or a shy person realizes that it would be advantageous to be more assertive. Many struggle, though, for two reasons: they want others to change first, and they think too globally. Let's look at each.

Ultimately change is an issue
between each person and God.

First, we would like to change if we can be assured that others will change. Is this strange? Not really. We are interdependent people by nature. We each derive a certain amount of motivation by knowing that we are not alone in our efforts. For example, a wife is likely to exercise greater patience when she knows the husband is willing to make an effort equal to hers.

But what do we do when others let us down? What if the spouse doesn't care about giving a reciprocal effort? What if extended family members continue to be oblivious to your growth? What if friends just advise you to shape up, giving no thought to their own need to change?

You can still move forward. Your efforts do not have to be contingent on others' initiatives. Granted, it would be better if all parties in your system had equal growth goals. That would be the fair thing. But then, fairness is not the paramount issue here.

Ultimately change is an issue between each person and God. As the Holy Spirit convicts us of matters to be altered, He then gives us the strength to make the adjustments. Different instruments can be used in the process—a Christian counselor, encouragement from a friend, wisdom from a book, an insightful seminar or sermon. But ultimately our change hinges on our willingness to deepen our spiritual lives, not on the behavior of others.

This concept has many implications for family and social networks. If your spouse if emotionally imbalanced, you can determine to be healthy in your responses. If your child is unruly, you are under no obligation to respond with your own unruly emotions. If a friend is insensitive, you can still determine to be guided by personal security.

Second, we tend to think too globally as we attempt to change. By this I mean that we can give ourselves broad, general goals that represent different behavior, but we lack immediate specifics. For instance, suppose you have a quick temper, so you tell yourself that you want to be more patient in all your interactions. That is too broad of a goal. Be specific. Remind yourself of the times you are most vulnerable to your temper and give yourself small assignments for brief increments of time. For example, at the end of the day you feel weary and you do not want to listen to the children's bickering. That is your vulnerable time. Give yourself the assignment of responding calmly to the children's responses for just one hour, no more. Or perhaps you feel defensive around a particular judgmental neighbor. When you are in that person's presence, give yourself the directive to make no defensive statements for a thirty minute stretch of time.

As your insights regarding the reasons for your emotions increase, you will feel confident in the effort to be different. But instead of making your goals too broad, you will apply them in the here and now.

The steps described in this chapter indicate that you can pull together the information presented in all the preceding chapters, with the goal of finding true success in your personal growth. Diligence is required. Focus is necessary. But as you yield to God's insights and plans, you can be assured that He will guide you toward a healthy life.